797,885 Books

are available to read at

Forgotten Books

www.ForgottenBooks.com

Forgotten Books' App
Available for mobile, tablet & eReader

ISBN 978-1-330-96839-0
PIBN 10127645

This book is a reproduction of an important historical work. Forgotten Books uses state-of-the-art technology to digitally reconstruct the work, preserving the original format whilst repairing imperfections present in the aged copy. In rare cases, an imperfection in the original, such as a blemish or missing page, may be replicated in our edition. We do, however, repair the vast majority of imperfections successfully; any imperfections that remain are intentionally left to preserve the state of such historical works.

Forgotten Books is a registered trademark of FB &c Ltd.
Copyright © 2015 FB &c Ltd.
FB &c Ltd, Dalton House, 60 Windsor Avenue, London, SW19 2RR.
Company number 08720141. Registered in England and Wales.

For support please visit www.forgottenbooks.com

1 MONTH OF FREE READING

at

www.ForgottenBooks.com

By purchasing this book you are eligible for one month membership to ForgottenBooks.com, giving you unlimited access to our entire collection of over 700,000 titles via our web site and mobile apps.

To claim your free month visit: www.forgottenbooks.com/free127645

* Offer is valid for 45 days from date of purchase. Terms and conditions apply.

English
Français
Deutsche
Italiano
Español
Português

www.forgottenbooks.com

Mythology Photography **Fiction**
Fishing Christianity **Art** Cooking
Essays **Buddhism** Freemasonry
Medicine **Biology** Music **Ancient Egypt** Evolution Carpentry Physics
Dance Geology **Mathematics** Fitness
Shakespeare **Folklore** Yoga Marketing
Confidence Immortality Biographies
Poetry **Psychology** Witchcraft
Electronics Chemistry History **Law**
Accounting **Philosophy** Anthropology
Alchemy Drama Quantum Mechanics
Atheism Sexual Health **Ancient History**
Entrepreneurship Languages Sport
Paleontology Needlework Islam
Metaphysics Investment Archaeology
Parenting Statistics Criminology
Motivational

NOTES

ON THE

BEDOUINS AND WAHÁBYS,

COLLECTED

DURING HIS TRAVELS IN THE EAST,

BY THE LATE

JOHN LEWIS BURCKHARDT.

PUBLISHED BY AUTHORITY OF
THE ASSOCIATION FOR PROMOTING THE DISCOVERY OF
THE INTERIOR OF AFRICA.

IN TWO VOLUMES.

VOL. II.

LONDON:
HENRY COLBURN AND RICHARD BENTLEY,
NEW BURLINGTON STREET.
1831.

PRINTED BY A. J. VALPY, RED LION COURT, FLEET STREET.

OF THE SECOND VOLUME.

ACCOUNT OF THE BEDOUIN TRIBES.

	PAGE
Additions to the Classification of Bedouin Tribes	1
Horses of Arabia	50
Camels	68
Locusts	89

MATERIALS FOR A HISTORY OF THE WAHABYS.

Introduction	95
Of Saoud's person and family	120
Wahaby Government	131
Administration of Justice	135
Revenues	151
Military Affairs of the Wahabys	162
Ghaleb, Sherif of Mekka, and the Turkish Pasha of Baghdád, at war with the Wahábys—The holy cities, Mekka and Medinah, taken by the Wahábys	180

Mohammed Aly, Pasha of Cairo, despatches his son, Tousoun Pasha, with a Turkish army to invade

CONTENTS.

	PAGE
Arabia—Thomas Keith, a Scotchman, (Ibrahím Aga,) commander of Tousoun's Mammelouks—His intrepidity—Ahmed Aga, surnamed Bonaparte—Medinah taken by the Turks, and Mekka surrendered to them	218
Mohammed Aly Pasha proceeds from Egypt with an army of Turks—Arrives at Djidda and Mekka—Arrests Sherif Ghaleb, and sends him prisoner to Cairo—Ghaleb's troops assemble at Taraba	246
The Begoum Arabs headed by a woman, regarded as a sorceress by the Turks, who are defeated at Taraba—Mohammed Aly takes Gonfode—Discontent of the Turkish troops—Death of Saoud—His son Abdallah declared chief of the Wahábys	268
Distribution of the Turkish forces in Hedjaz—Massacre at Bahra—Mohammed Aly sends his son Tousoun Pasha to Medinah—The Turks defeated by the Wahábys in Zohrán—Mohammed Aly marches from Mekka towards Byssel—The Wahábys defeated there	290
Turks elated with victory—their cruelty—their distresses on the march from Beishe—Mohammed Aly returns to Mekka—Makes proposals of peace to Abdallah Ibn Saoud	322
Abdallah Ibn Saoud enters Kasym with an army—Negotiations between him and Tousoun Pasha—Peace concluded—Mohammed Aly returns to Cairo—Despatches his son, Ibrahím Pasha, with an army to renew the war in Hedjaz	342
Appendix, (comprising six articles)	361
Index of Arabic words	379

ACCOUNT

OF

THE BEDOUINS.

ADDITIONS TO THE CLASSIFICATION OF BEDOUIN TRIBES.

A CONSIDERABLE portion of the *Wold Aly* tribe reside above *Khaibar*, in the Southern Desert of Arabia.

The tribe of *el Hessenne*.—Their chief is named *Mehanna*, having been born in the "low-grounds," so called in the Desert, between Tedmor and Anah. Those low grounds, which are denominated "wádys," and of which the Bedouins distinguish eight as the principal in this direction, are the pasturing places of all the great Aeneze tribes in winter time, and extend for a distance of five days' journeys from west to east. Wady Hauran, which has been mentioned in a preceding account of this Desert, forms a part of those wadys. During the last century this ground was the continual scene of conflict between the Mowaly Arabs, who were then very powerful, but at present inhabit the desert about Aleppo, and the Beni Khaled tribe from Basra. On those grounds both tribes were accustomed to meet in winter, and contend for the right of pasture.

The Djelás, or el Rowalla.

This third branch of the great Aeneze nation is not properly named Rowalla, but *Djelás*, and these are divided into two principal tribes.

1. *El Rowalla* (a name which should not be applied to the whole branch): their minor tribes are *el Ktaysán, el Doghama, el Feregge,* and *el Naszyr*.

2. The *Omhallef*, whose sheikh is *el Maadjel*.—To these belong the tribes of *Abdelle, Fersha, el Bedour,* and *el Sowaleme*.

Most of the great Aeneze tribes, as I have already remarked, are entitled to passage-money from the Syrian hadj, or pilgrim caravan. Thus, for instance, the El Ahsenne take a yearly *surra* or tribute of fifty purses (or about one thousand pounds), dividing it among a number of their individuals. A surra to the same amount is taken by the Wold Aly. The Fedán, who at present are one of the strongest Aeneze tribes, receive nothing from the pilgrims.

The Djelás were, in former times, perpetually wandering about Nedjd. They are known in Syria principally, since the battle which they fought with the Baghdad troops in the year 1809, upon a piece of ground formed into a corner or angle by the river Euphrates and the Khabour, opposite to Rahaba. Having taken several small guns and some tents, they carried them to Derayeh, the capital. About five hundred horses which became their property as plunder, they sold to Asyr Arabs of Yemen. Those Djelás are the most wild and warlike tribe of the Desert between Syria and Basra. By their great numbers and strength, they have latterly been enabled to extort tribute from many Syrian villages.

The Besher, or Bisher.

These divide themselves into two great branches.

1. The *Tana Mádjed* Arabs, to whom belong, as minor tribes, the *Fedán* and the *Sebaa*.

2. The *Selga* Arabs. Of these the greater part occupy the district of *el Hassa* on the Persian Gulf, belonging to the Wahabys. Of those Selgas there are three ramifications, the *Medheyán, Metarafe,* and the considerable tribe called *Oulád Soleymán.* The Selga sheikh is Ibn Haddal, a strenuous supporter of the Wahabys. He was present in almost every battle fought from the year 1812 to 1815 in Hedjaz against the army of Mohammed Aly; and it was chiefly through his exertions that Tousoun Pasha was kept completely in check on his progress in spring, 1815, from Medinah towards Kasym.

The *Fedan* Arabs have latterly become

very powerful, and defeated the Hessenne under Mehanna in many encounters on the Syrian frontier.

The *Oulad Soleymán* are descendants from the ancient tribe of *Djaafere*, which is now almost extinct. Another small tribe claiming descent also from Djaafere is named *Owádje*. These people generally encamp with the Wold Aly in Hauran, and occupy above two hundred tents; they do not belong to the nation of the Aenezes. Of these Djaafere, a part went over to Egypt at the time of the Muselman conquest; their descendants are now settled on the western banks of the Nile in Upper Egypt, among the numerous villages between Esna and Assouán. It may be remarked as an extraordinary circumstance, that the women descended from this tribe of Djaafere are celebrated both in Egypt and Arabia for their frequent production of twins. The usual dwelling-place of the Oulad Soleyman is on the vicinity of Khaibar; they constitute a very strong and warlike tribe, occupying about five thousand tents.

The Sebaa Arabs, who at present live on the Syrian frontiers, had their residences formerly in Nedjd. They left that country about twelve years ago, that they might be less exposed to the extortions of the Wahaby chief.

Ahl el Shemál.

This denomination is used by the Syrian Arabs only with relation to their own position. Among the Arabs of Hedjáz, the whole Aeneze tribe is classed among the *Ahl el Shemál,* or " northern nations." The great ancestor of the Aenezes was *Wayl,* and his descendants, the Beni Wayl, are known in historical records as the contemporaries and the enemies of Mohammed. Not much more than one hundred and twenty years have now elapsed since the Aenezes came from Khaibar and Nedjd into Syria. For the extraordinary increase of this numerous nation and their great abundance of cattle, the Bedouins account in the following manner. They relate that Wayl, their illustrious forefather, by some fortunate chance happened to ascertain the exact moment of the *Leilet el Kader* (the twenty-fifth or twenty-seventh night of the fast Ramadhan), when the Almighty is always disposed to comply with the prayers of mortals. Wayl, placing his hands on certain parts of his she-camel and of his own person, implored the divine blessing, with respect to those objects which he touched: his prayers were favourably heard; he was blest with a numerous family of sons and daughters; and his people became rich in a multiplicity of camels. This story is related and firmly believed by every person of the Aeneze tribe.

El Mowaly.—The celebrated sheikh of this tribe, *El Gendj*, one of the bravest men in Syria, was treacherously killed by the Pasha of Aleppo in his own *harám*, in the year 1818; and his son, a boy of sixteen, invested with the office of guardian of the Desert of Aleppo. They were formerly sole masters of the open country about Aleppo and Hamah, and were entitled to a considerable *surra*, or annual tribute, from the hadj of pilgrims passing through their territory. Of these advantages they have been dispossessed by the Aenezes, and are now reduced to small numbers, and very limited extent of patrimony.

The *Fehely* Arabs of Damascus are certain tribes who labour under the imputation of being persons of bad faith; and in general it is found that this unfavourable opinion, which all the Bedouins entertain respecting them, is but too justly applicable to numerous individuals among them. They endeavour to extenuate their faults by an exercise of hospitality. Thus in Syria, the Mowalys and Fehelys are notorious for treachery; but, on the other hand, are celebrated for treating their guests with a profusion of victuals. The Fehelys, in particular, are despised, because they do not scruple to steal from the tents of their friends.

The *Howeytât* derive their origin from the ancient tribe of *Beni Atye*; from whom likewise are descended the *Heywât* (also entitled *Leheywât*), the *Terabein*, the *Maazy* (in the desert between Suez and Cosseir), and the *Tyaha*. Those Arab tribes dwelling on the eastern gulf of the Red Sea, generally receive their supplies of provisions from the country about Khalyl. Should the harvest in Syria not have been abundant, those Arabs travel a journey of fourteen or fifteen days to Cairo, and there furnish themselves with the necessary stock of corn.

The *Omran*, although connected by alliance with the Howeytát, do not in fact belong to them, but form a distinct tribe in themselves. They inhabit the mountains between Akaba and Moeyleh, on the eastern coast of the Red Sea. The Omran are a strong tribe of very independent spirit. Their frequent depredations render them objects of terror to the pilgrims proceeding to Mekka, who are under the necessity of passing through their territory. At the time when Mohammed Aly, Pasha of Egypt, had reduced all other Bedouins on the Egyptian hadj road to complete subjection, the Omran still proved obstinate. In the year 1814 they attacked and plundered a detachment of Turkish cavalry near Akaba; and in 1815 they pillaged the whole advanced corps of the Syrian pilgrim caravan, on their return from Medinah to Damascus. Among their principal tribes are the *Hadnán*.

The *Debour* and *Bedoul* are tribes that reside in the vicinity of the Akaba; they are in alliance with the tribes of Omran and Howeytat: in the same quarter also dwell the *Seyayhe*.

Among the Arabs of Khalyl, or Hebron, are, *el Tyáha*—whose principal tribe is called *el Hekouk*—the *Terabein*—who conduct the caravans from Ghaza and Hebron to Suez; of their tribes one is the *Azazeme*—the *Wahydy* (or *Wahydát*), among whose tribes are the *Oulad el Fokora*. There is also a small tribe about Ghaza and Hebron, called *Reteymát*, and another, the *Khanasera*. These Arabs of Ghaza and Khalyl repair in spring time to the borders of the canals on the river Nile, in the Sherkieh, where they pasture their cattle on the fine herbage produced by the inundation.

The Arabs of Tor, or Towara.

These inhabit the peninsula of Sinai, and are divided into three branches—the *Sowaleha*, *Mezeyne*, and *Aleygat*.

1. The *Sowaleha*, who are subdivided into four tribes, viz.—the *Oulad Sayd*, the *Owareme*, the *Gerāshy*, and the *Rahamy*. Those whom I have here named *Gerāshy* are descended from the ancient *Gereysh* of Mekka, as the Arabs pronounce the name قريش, which Europeans generally express by *Koreish*. The Sowaleha can muster about three hundred matchlocks, but they have not any horses, and, like all the Towara tribes, maintain very little intercourse with their eastern neighbours.

2. The *Mezeyne*—descended from a tribe of the same name residing eastward of Medinah. The Mezeyne and Aleygát tribes remain in the eastern and southern parts of the peninsula.

3. The *Aleygát*. These, with the Mezeyne tribe, can form together a force of three hundred matchlocks. The Aleygáts settled in Nubia, below *Derr*, are acknowledged by the Sinai Aleygáts to be of the same original stock. Besides the three tribes above mentioned, the Tyaha and Terabein likewise pasture their flocks in the northern parts of the peninsula of Mount Sinai. There are rem-

nants of two tribes found in this country, originally from Barbary; the *Beni Wászel* and the *Beni Soleymán*. Some of the Beni Wászel live in Upper Egypt, on the eastern bank of the Nile, opposite Mirriet, where they have become cultivators. None of the Tor Bedouins have at present any horses.

To complete this review of the Eastern Bedouins, the names of those tribes that wander about in the neighbourhood of the eastern frontiers of the Egyptian Delta are subjoined—

Arabs of the Sherkyeh of Egypt.

These were once very powerful tribes, which the fertility of the country had attracted from various parts. During the time of the Mamelouk reign in Egypt, it might be said that they were the sole masters in the province of *Sherkyeh:* they exacted a tribute from all the villages; indeed many villages belonged to them, so that the peasants were obliged to divide the produce with these owners. The confined space of ground in which they moved, and their intermixture with the peasants (to whom they bestow their girls in marriage), rendered the conquest of them more easy to Mohammed Aly, Pasha of Egypt, who not only subdued, but almost wholly exterminated them; in doing which he very materially served his own Egyptians, who had been always extremely ill-treated by those tribes, of whom the principal are:—

El Sowaleha—related to those of the Sinai peninsula above noticed.

The *Ayayde*, who about one hundred years ago formed a tribe of six hundred horsemen. They sometimes encamp in the mountains between Suez and Cosseir, but are more commonly found in the flat country not far from Cairo. They occupy about one hundred tents; their minor tribes are, *Salatene, Djerabene* and *Maazy*, but these must not be confounded with others bearing the same name. The Ayayde are perpetually at enmity with the Howeytát. Some of their encampments are seen on the Syrian road, leading towards El Arish.

The *Howeytát* — related to those of the east, but become so degenerate in consequence of their intermixture with the peasants that they can scarcely be distinguished from them. They are principally engaged in the transport business between Cairo and Suez. Their branch-tribes are, *el Mowalle, Ghanayme, Shedayde, Zeráyne*, amounting all together to about six hundred tents.

The *Heteym.*—Of this wide-spread nation, of which individuals are found in every corner of Arabia, considerable numbers have reached Upper Egypt, where they encamp above *Gous*, and *Goft*, or Coptos.

The *Djeheyne.*—These came from Hedjaz, where their main tribe still exists.

The *Bily*—likewise eastern: all these tribes come either as fugitives, or for the purpose of benefiting by the advantages which robbers may derive from the neighbourhood of so rich a country as Egypt. These Arabs of the Sherkyeh have all (with the exception of the Maazy) adopted the Egyptian dialect; and this circumstance alone would be sufficient to render them despicable in the opinion of all true Arabian Bedouins. The small Bedouin tribes of Syria, on the contrary, who were never out of the inhabited parts, surrounded by Syrian peasants, still retain the Bedouin dialect in all its purity. The Bedouins of Syria have never mixed so much with the inhabitants of that country as the Egyptian Bedouins have done with the Fellahs, among whom they reside.

The *Aleygât*—a kindred tribe of those in the mountains of Sinai. They derive their origin from the Syrian Desert.

The *Azayre*, belonging to the *Heteym*. Several camps of the Azayre are found in Upper Egypt.

The tribe of *Amarât*.

The *Maazy*. These sometimes pasture their flocks near the Nile, but generally reside in the mountains between Cairo and Cosseir; they are most commonly employed in the transport trade between Cosseir and Genne. These Maazy are the only Egyptians of their race who have preserved the language, dress, manners, and institutions of the Eastern Bedouins in all their original purity. They were formerly stationed southward and eastward of the Omrán, about Moeyleh, where their brethren still remain. In the course of the last century, having been much annoyed by various enemies, they abandoned their homes and sought refuge in Egypt. Those who undertook their journey by land, were, for the greater number, killed during their passage through the territory of the Howeytats. Others came over by sea to Tor, and arrived safely in Egypt, where, finding that the Sherkye was fully peopled with Bedouins, they retired to the mountains eastward of the river Nile. Having been frequently at war with the Beys of Egypt, and latterly with the *Pasha*, their numbers are considerably reduced. At present, the utmost of their force does not exceed two hundred horsemen. They are constantly at variance with the Ababde Bedouins, who reside on the south of the Cosseir route. Within the last twenty or thirty years, those Sherkye tribes have been rendered more numerous by the addition of—

The *Hanády*, a tribe of Moggrebyn Bedouins, who have adopted the dress and customs of the Barbary and Libyan Arabs. They were formerly established in the Beheyre province of the Delta, and in the Desert extending from the Pyramids towards

Alexandria Having been overpowered by the Oulad Aly, another Moggrebyn tribe of the same province, much superior to them in numbers, they were obliged to abandon the right of tribute which they had exacted from the villages of Beheyre, and leaving it to their more powerful rivals, they retired across the river Nile towards the Sherkye, where they now reside. From five to six hundred horsemen constitute the utmost force of all those Sherkye tribes. Thirty years ago they were able to muster at least three thousand, if we may believe their own reports. The Pasha of Egypt levies a tribute on them at present, and observes their movements with so much vigilance that they are not even permitted to make war against each other; the most galling predicament in which a Bedouin can possibly be placed. The district between Belbeis and Salehye is the most frequented by these Bedouins, to whose number may be added the three tribes, *el Howámede, Oulad Mousa,* and *Lebádye.*

Returning from the limits of Egypt towards the eastern borders of the Red Sea, I shall continue to trace the different tribes as far south as Mekka and Tayf.

The *Howeytât* and *Omrân*, (who have been already mentioned) extend as far as the neighbourhood of Moeyleh. Among them, in the mountains not very remote from the sea, are likewise some encampments of the Bily and Heteym tribes; and at a distance of two days' journies southward of Akaba, in the fertile wady called *Megna*, which is remarkable for its abundance of date-trees, reside the Megana Arabs, who are partly husbandmen or cultivators.

Eastward of Akaba and Megna, towards the Syrian hadj road, we find the *Maazy* tribe, who are in a state of constant warfare with the Omran. They constitute a force of about four or perhaps five hundred matchlocks, and are the brethren of the Egyptian Maazys.

The *Beni Okaba*, the same as that tribe which inhabits the vicinity of Kerek; they possess the small town of Moeyleh and the surrounding country. Parties of the Mesayd Arabs are likewise found in the neighbourhood of Moeyleh.

El Bily. These Arabs inhabit the country between Moeyleh and the castle of *Wodje,* and the wady bearing the same name, a principal station on the hadj road, being abundantly supplied with excellent water. The castle of Wodje is situated on the mountain, about three miles distant from the sea, where there is a good harbour; the garrison consists of about a dozen Moggrebyn soldiers: this seems to be the original abode of the Bily: those of the same tribe who live in Syria and Egypt are *advenæ.* In spring time many of these Arabs cross with their sheep and goats in small boats over to the islands within sight of the shore, where the winter rains have produced vegetation, and continue there as long as they can find rain-water remaining in the rocks of these islands. Some Howeytáts are found southward of Moeyleh; they are called *Howeytát el Kebly,* to distinguish them from their brethren of the north.

Heteym. To the distance of three days' journies from Wodje, in a southern direction as far as the promontory and mountain of *Hassány,* the country is inhabited by the Heteyms. Of the innumerable tribes who people the deserts of Arabia, none is more dispersed, nor more frequently seen in all parts of that country, than the Heteym. In Syria, in Lower and Upper Egypt, along the whole coast of the Red Sea down to Yemen, in Nedjd and Mesopotamia, encampments of the Heteym are always to be found. Perhaps it is from this wandering disposition that they are much less respected than any other tribe. For one Bedouin to call another " Heteymy," is considered as a very serious insult; for the Heteyms are despised as a mean race of people, and in most provinces the other Bedouins will not intermarry with them. They are, besides, obliged almost every where, to pay tribute to the neighbouring Bedouins for permission to pasture their cattle; and I believe that, with the exception of this territory bordering on the Red Sea, where the property of the land is peculiarly their own, they are no where regarded as owners of the place which they inhabit, while the contrary is the case with all genuine and true-born Bedouins. Thus in Egypt, Syria, and Hedjaz, the Heteyms pay a tribute in sheep to all their neighbours. Conscious of the little esteem in which they are universally held, these Heteyms have renounced all their martial spirit, and have become of a peaceable character, but extremely shuffling, which renders them still more disliked.

The Heteym women have the reputation of being very beautiful, and licentious in their manners; and the Arabs say that the slave of a Heteymy will never attempt to run away, because his mistress never hesitates about admitting him to her embraces. It must, however, be allowed, that the Heteyms are commended for generous conduct and hospitality towards strangers; but these virtues have been forced upon them by the necessity of endeavouring to conciliate, in some degree, the amity of their neighbours. Like all the other Bedouins on this coast, they are active fishermen: they sell their dried fish to the crews of ships coming from, or going to Hedjaz. The Heteyms also fish for pearls near several of the islands. They purchase their provision of corn at Moeyleh and Wodje; but they live principally on milk, meat, fish, and wild honey. They possess but few camels, and are altogether without horses; but their flocks of sheep are very numerous, and they take them for sale to Tor and Yembo. In general the Bedouins on this side of the Red Sea are poor, because their land does not afford good pasturage; and they live at such a distance from towns, that no advantage can be derived from any intercourse with the inhabitants.

The *Beni Abs.*—A few families of this ancient and celebrated tribe, among which the famous Antar was educated, still continue to inhabit the Djebel Hassany, (from three to four days' journey north of Yembo,) and an island opposite to it, called *el Harra*. They are the only Bedouins of Arabia who preserve the name of *Abs*; although there still exist many tribes who claim descent from that illustrious nation, but are known by other denominations. Like the Heteyms, these people of the Abs tribe are held in much disrepute; and the name of *Absy* is applied to a stranger with the intention of insulting him, in the same manner as the name of *Heteymy*. The Abs possess several small ships, in which they carry provisions to Hedjaz and Suez; and when the rains cease, they pasture their few sheep upon the island of *Harra* above mentioned. In the beginning of the last century these Abs were still a numerous tribe: even at present, the few remaining families of them are entitled to a tribute from the Egyptian pilgrim caravan; a tribute which, in very remote ages, their ancestors had enforced.

Djeheyney.—To the south of Djebel Hassany (northward of Yembo as above described), begin the dwelling places of the great tribe of *Djeheyne*, extending along the sea-coast as far as below Yembo, and eastward to Hedye, a station of the Syrian hadj road. From Yembo, in the direction of Medinah these Djeheyne possess the ground to a distance of about twelve or fifteen hours. The cultivated vallies of *Yembo el Nakhel* also belong to them. Part of this tribe are cultivators, but the greater number continue Bedouins. They constitute the chief portion of the population of Yembo; and although they possess but a few horses, it is said that they can muster a force amounting to eight thousand matchlocks. They are constantly at war with the neighbouring tribe of Beni Harb;

through whose assistance the Wahaby chief, Saoud, was enabled to subjugate them, while all the other tribes above mentioned, southward of Akaba, had invariably refused to submit; and Saoud had not thought it expedient to attack them in their mountains, contenting himself with detaching occasionally some plundering parties against them. The Djeheynes nominally acknowledge the supremacy of the Sherif of Mekka: they proved very serviceable to the Pasha of Egypt at the taking of Medinah, in the year 1812.

Like all the Bedouins before mentioned, dwelling southward of Akaba, the Djeheyne are entitled to surra, or passage money, from the pilgrims of the Egyptian hadj. Of their branch tribes I cannot give any account.

Returning to the latitude of Akaba, I shall now proceed to enumerate the Bedouin tribes of the Eastern Desert, towards Nedjd, and thence on to Medinah.

Bedouins of the Desert between Akaba el Shámy (or the Syrian Akaba) and Medinah comprising those of Nedjd.

I can speak of these tribes merely from hearsay, and well-authenticated reports, while I myself have seen individuals of almost every other tribe enumerated in these pages, from the river Euphrates, down to Mekka and Tayf. The tribes which I am now about to describe are all Wahabys, continuing to profess themselves such even after the campaign of Mohammed Aly Pasha against these sectarians.

The Desert southward of Akaba, as far as Hedjer, is almost wholly inhabited by Aenezes. But the watering-places of that Desert are few, and on that account the Bedouins seldom remain stationary on the hadj route, but take up their abode in the eastern parts, towards Djebel Shammar, and Kasym. The Aeneze tribes encamped in these districts are—

The *Oulad Soleymán*, a tribe of Besher:

they have about five thousand tents in the neighbourhood of Khaibar.

The *Rowalla* of the *Djelás*, who are likewise established at Khaibar.

El Fokara, belonging to the Wold Aly, at Hedjer—These Fokara are much celebrated for their bravery. All the tribes here mentioned are rich in horses, and exact a tribute from the pilgrim caravan.

Bedouins of Djebel Shammar.

The *Beni Shammar*—whose sheikh, Ibn Aly, is a man of considerable influence at the Wahaby court. These Beni Shammar possess but few horses; they are, however, able to muster from three thousand to four thousand men, all armed with matchlocks. Some of them are Bedouins, and others cultivators. Part of their tribe is in Mesopotamia, where they have always proved themselves great enemies of the Wahabys.

The most numerous branch of the Beni Shammar are the *Degheyfát*.

El Djaafar.

El Rebaay—These are descended from the ancient tribe of *Beni Deyghám;* whose chief, Orar el Deyghámi, is often mentioned in Bedouin tales.

The *Zegeyrát*—descended from the same Beni Deygham, are cultivators in the vicinity of Imam Hosseyn. There are in the Djebel Shammar and Nedjd several other Bedouin tribes, besides those above mentioned, but I have not been able to ascertain their names.

Bedouins of Kasym, and other parts of Nedjd.

There is scarcely any great tribe of the Arabian Desert which has not always some encampment in Nedjd. The inhabitants of all the towns and villages in that country are descended from Bedouin tribes, whom they much resemble in their manners and institutions. Of those tribes who wander about this part of the country during the whole year are—

The *Selga*—one of the great branches of the Bisher Arabs, belonging to the Aenezes.

Their chief, Ibn Haddal, a man in high favour with the Waháby government.

The *Sahhoun*—celebrated for their bravery and activity as horsemen; of whom they can muster to the number of three hundred.

The *Beni Lam*—related to those bearing the same name, who pasture their flocks on the banks of the Shat el Arab: they form but a small tribe.

The *Heteym.*— Here we again find this tribe, as every where else throughout Arabia.

The *Beni Hosseyn*—a tribe of wandering Arabs, who, like the Persians, are disciples of Aly. They professed to adopt the Wahaby doctrines, but continued secretly attached to their Persian, or *Shya*, creed.

The *Zaab*—an inconsiderable tribe, residing in Nedjd and El Hassa.

The *Ageyl.*—In former ages these were a very powerful tribe, descended from the Beni Helál. They now are scattered about in small numbers among the villages of Nedjd. But another tribe called also Beni Ageyl, has lately sprung up since the reign of Sultan Murad. All the Arabs of Nedjd, whether settlers or Bedouins, who repair to Baghdad, and establish themselves there, become members of the tribe of Ageyl of Baghdad, which enjoys considerable influence at that place, and is, in fact, the strongest support of the Pasha in his wars with the surrounding Bedouins, and against the rebels of that city. The chief of these Ageyls of Baghdad is always some native of Derayeh, chosen from among themselves, and confirmed by the Pasha. These Ageyls are celebrated for their bravery. They conduct the caravans from Baghdad to Syria, and have frequently repulsed very superior forces of the Wahabys. They divide themselves into two classes at Baghdad.

1. The *Zogorty*—comprising the poorer individuals and pedlars.

2. The *Djemamyl*, who conduct the caravans. Among these classes of Ageyls are found persons belonging to many different tribes and districts, such as El Hassa, El Aaredh, El Kasym, and Djebel Shammar. Those settlers of the *Zedeyr* district (forming part of Nedjd,) who come to Baghdad, are not admitted as members of this body. Individuals of the southern tribe of Dowasyr, near

the frontiers of Yemen, are likewise not to be found among these Ageyls.

Meteyr (or, as they are sometimes denominated, *Emteyr*).—These are a strong tribe, consisting of twelve hundred horsemen, and from six to eight thousand matchlocks. They live in Nedjd, chiefly in Kasym, and from thence on towards Medinah. They branch off into four principal tribes—1. The *Alowa*, whose sheikh, Dowysh, was an ally of Tousoun Pasha in his wars with the Wahabys. 2. The *Boráy*; their sheikh is called Merykhy. 3. *El Harabeshe;* and 4. *El Borsán.* Some of the Meteyr are likewise to be found in Mesopotamia : they are all inveterate enemies of the Aenezes.

From Kasym towards Medinah and Mekka.

Except the space occupied by the Meteyr, and some encampments of the Heteym, this whole extent of country is inhabited by the mighty tribe of *Harb,* which in numbers only yields to the Aenezes, and next to them constitutes the most formidable association of Bedouins in Arabia.

The Beni Harb.*

From the aggregate of this tribe, there might probably be formed a body comprising between thirty and forty thousand men armed with matchlocks; and such is the numerical strength of their main tribes, that each of them is rather to be considered as a distinct body; yet the ties which connect the whole body together are much stronger than those by which the numerous Aeneze tribes are united. Some of the Harbs are settlers; some are Bedouins. Almost every tribe has adopted both modes of life. They derive considerable profit from the Syrian and Egyptian pilgrim caravans, and may be styled the masters of Hedjaz. They were the last tribe in these countries that yielded to the Wahabys. They have few horses southward of Medinah, but every boy is armed with a matchlock. The Arabs belonging to this tribe of Harb frequently make plundering excursions

* It may be here remarked that the word *Harb* in Arabic signifies "war."

against the Aenezes in their camps, as far as the plains of Hauran near Damascus.

Of the Harb tribe, east of Medinah, are

The *Mezeyne*, who can muster between four and five hundred horsemen, and about two thousand matchlocks. These became Wahabys long before the other tribes of Harb submitted: they are all Bedouins.

The *Wohoub*, and the *Gharbán*.

The *Djenáyne.*—Some of these are settlers, and cultivators of fields among the hills eastward of Medinah to the distance of between two and three days' journies: from this they probably derive their name.

Beni Aly.—These are of the Persian creed, and followers of Aly. In numbers they amount to five hundred matchlocks. A few of them are settlers. They possess some watering-places, situated in fertile spots, where they sow corn and barley; but continue to live under tents, and pass the greater part of the year in the Desert.

Of the Harb tribe near Medinah, eastward and southward.

Beni Safar—Beni Ammer. This is a tribe amounting to between two and three thousand matchlocks, and three hundred horsemen; they live on the east and south of Medinah, and have the character of being cowardly and of bad faith; many of them are cultivators. The district of *El Fera*, (from which dates are exported all over Hedjaz, and which is said to be very fertile,) is in their possession. Their sheikh, Dofny, first joined the Turkish army, but in Kasym went over again to the Wahabys.

El Hámede—Likewise on the east and south of Medinah; equal in strength to the Beni Safar above mentioned. Among them very few are cultivators; their sheikh, Mohammed Ibn Motlab, is considered at present as chief of all the Beni Harb. He succeeded to Djezye, who was treacherously murdered at Medinah, in the year 1814, by the Turkish governor.

The Beni Harb between Medinah and Mekka are entitled to a considerable tribute, or surra, from the Syrian as well as from the Egyptian hadj caravan. The tribute of the latter is said to be about eight thousand dollars, which the sheikhs divide among themselves and many individuals.

The Harb, southward of Medinah.

The *Beni Salem* — Among the vallies of Djedeyde and Safra, where they live in houses amidst plantations of date-trees; but few of these are Bedouins. They muster two thousand five hundred matchlocks, and are reported to be excellent soldiers; they receive a considerable tribute from the Syrian hadj, as the pilgrims belonging to it pass through their territory.

The *Howáseb*, to whom belongs *el Hamra*, a village with fields and gardens, between Djedeyde and Safra. The greater part of these Howáseb are Bedouins.

The *Sobh*.—These can assemble two thousand five hundred men, armed with matchlocks, and reckoned the most warlike among the tribes of Harb. To them belong **Beder**, and the surrounding country. I have seen them sit during the day-time in their small shops at Beder (where a market is held), and in the evening mount their camels that they might return to their families in the Desert. Some of them are permanently settled at Beder; the greater number inhabit the mountain of *Sobh*, eastward of Beder, which is inaccessible to enemies, and was the refuge of the Harb tribe against the Wahabys, who could never dislodge them from it. Upon that mountain grows the balm-tree and Senna in great abundance. They subdivide themselves into the three tribes of *Shokbân*, *Rehalát*, and *Khadhera*.

El Owf, the wildest of the Harb tribes. They occupy the mountains southward of Djebel Sobh toward Rábegh, and were never completely subjugated by the Wahabys. The name of Owf is dreaded as far as Mekka, and particularly by all pilgrims; for they are most enterprising robbers, and parties of them amounting to three or four hundred men have been known to carry off at night, by force, valuable loads out of the midst of the encampments of the hadj. They are accustomed to follow the hadj upon its return by night, to a distance of several days' journies beyond Medinah, in hopes of cutting off the stragglers.

El Haib, a branch of the Owf, has emigrated (as I have already mentioned) into Syria, and occupies with its camels the fertile pasture-ground on the summit of Mount Libanon.

Dwy Dhaher.—These extend from Rábegh towards Mekka. Several encampments of them are likewise found in the vicinity of Medinah; they occupy the country as far as Wády Fatme. Their sheikh, Ghánem, rendered considerable services to the Turkish army at Medinah.

Beni Harb (in the low country, or Tehama or el Ghor, between the Mountains and the Sea).

Zebeyde.—These are in possession of the coast from the vicinity of Yembo, down to Djidda and Leith. (From Djidda southward, in the direction of Leith, encampments of the Heteym may likewise be seen.) Of the

Zebeyde tribe many are settlers. The marketplace of Kholeys with its fertile neighbourhood, at the distance of two days' journies northward of Djidda is their principal station. But as their territory is in general poor, they are obliged to seek for other means of subsistence than what can be derived from pasture alone. They are very active as fishermen: many of them are sailors, and serve as pilots between Yembo and Djidda. Their intimate connexion with the inhabitants of the towns of Hedjaz, and the trade in which they engage, have caused the other tribes of Harb to look upon them with disdain. A man of the Sobh or Beni Sálem tribe would resent it as a serious insult if any one were to call him a "*Zebeyde.*" Some of that same tribe of Zebeyde are said to be established on the Shat el Arab, below Baghdad. Among the Harb, from Medinah to Mekka, horses are very scarce; a few only are in the possession of their principal persons.

With most of the Harb tribe above mentioned I was personally acquainted; and the names of others of the same nation were familiar to me, although I do not exactly recollect their respective places of residence, but have reason to think them in the latitude of Medinah; their names are, *Sedda, Djemmela,* and *Saadyn.*

Bedouins from Medinah towards Mekka and Tayf, eastward of the great chain of Mountains.

The *Beni Harb* reside upon those mountains, and westward of them, towards the sea. To the east of that chain are the plains inhabited by the powerful tribe of *Ateybe,* whose territory extends as far south as Tayf. Their pasturing grounds are excellent. They possess great abundance of camels and sheep: they have also horses, and are in good reputation for bravery, being constantly at war with all their neighbours. They were, before the time of the Wahabys, the most inveterate enemies of the Harb tribe, and derived profit from the pilgrims of the hadj, whenever they passed through their territory; there being two hadj routes—one in a western direction from Medinah to Mekka, through the Harb country—the other, in an eastern direction through their own. With their different branches I am not acquainted. Their force cannot be less than six thousand matchlocks, and may amount to ten thousand.

Bedouins of Mekka.

Between Mekka and Djidda live the Bedouins called *Lahhyán*: these are related to the Hodheyl and Metarefe, and occupy the two principal stations on that road, *Hadda* and *Bahza*, places where a few of them reside in huts, and where travellers halt. The others pasture their flocks in the neighbouring mountains. Altogether they can muster about two hundred and fifty matchlocks. The Bedouins about Mekka are all poor, from the sterility of the ground which they inhabit, and the high price of all commodities and provisions in that country. Those of Tayf are much more at their ease.

*From Mekka southward, in Tehama, or the
"Low Country."*

Here dwell the *Beni Fahem*, who supply Mekka with charcoal and sheep. They are celebrated for having retained in its purity the Arabic language. Of men armed with matchlocks they can assemble about three hundred.

The *Beni Djehádele* occupy the country southward of the Fahem, towards Wady Lemlem. In time of peace they conduct the caravans from Mekka to the coast of Yemen.

From Mekka eastward, in the direction of the great chain of Mountains.

In the Wady Fatme, and Wady Zeyme or Wady Lymoun, reside some Sherifs of the Sherif families of Mekka, belonging to the tribe of Dwy Barakát, who cultivate those fertile vallies, and encamp likewise in the neighbouring desert.

The *Koreysh*.—Of this famous tribe only

three hundred matchlock-men now remain: they encamp about Mount Arafât. Notwithstanding their great name and ancient celebrity, they are but little esteemed by the other Bedouins. Mekka derives from them supplies of milk and butter.

The *Ryshye*.—This is a small tribe: it cannot muster above eighty matchlocks. The Ryshye engage in the transport trade between Mekka and Djidda. They are of recent origin, a kind of *advenæ*, held in little repute. Their small camps are pitched in the Wady Noman, on the way from Arafât towards Tayf; and in that wady they cultivate some fields.

The *Kabákebe*.—These reside in the vicinity of Sheddád, a station beyond Arafât, eastward; their numbers amount to about one hundred and fifty matchlocks.

The *Adouán*.—About forty years ago these formed a considerable tribe, mustering one thousand matchlocks. Their continual wars with every neighbour had reduced them to little more than one hundred families, and latterly they have been nearly exterminated by Mohammed Aly Pasha. They were an ancient and noble tribe, unequalled by any in Hedjaz for bravery and hospitality, and they occupied the first rank in public esteem. They were the intimate friends of the Sherifs of Mekka. The reigning Sherif, and all the families of the other Sherifs, were accustomed to send their children when eight days old to be educated among Bedouins, and principally among the tribe of Adouán, with whom they remained until they had learned to manage a horse with dexterity. It is well known that Mohammed himself was brought up in a similar manner among the tribe of Beni Sad. Their present system of politics has made them hostile to Mekka. Their late sheikh, Othman el Medhayfe, the brother-in-law of Sherif Ghaleb (who took him prisoner and beheaded him at Constantinople), had been named, by the Wahabys, chief of all the Bedouins of Mekka and Tayf. On his death the tribe fell into decay; and the few remaining families of the Adouáns have taken refuge among the Ateybes.

The Adouáns formerly had not any fixed pasturing places, but encamped all over the country from Djidda to Tayf. Such was their high reputation, that a man of the Hodheyl tribe said to me one day, "Where shall we now look for models of generosity and courage, since the Adouáns are gone?" A small branch of this tribe, called *el Harreth*, were all Sherifs, of the Beni Hashem race. In Nedjd also are found some branches of those Adouáns, not very numerous, but bearing the same names.

Bedouins of Tayf.

These are comprised under the denomination of *Thekyf*, and among them the Hodheyl are sometimes reckoned; but in general the Hodheyl are not included under that title.

The *Hodheyl* occupy the steep mountainous region on the road from Mekka to Tayf, and especially about the *Djebel Kora*. They muster one thousand matchlocks, and are reputed the best marksmen in the whole country. They are a famous tribe, eminent for their bravery. The Wahabys killed above three hundred of their best men before the tribe would submit. They have but few horses or camels; their sheep and goats, however, are numerous. They are subdivided into the three small tribes of *Alowyein*, *Nedowyein*, and *Beni Khaled*.

The *Toweyrek*. These live southward of the Hodheyl upon the same mountain: in numbers they amount to about five hundred matchlocks. They have the character of being expert thieves; which charge is not made against the Hodheyl, although these latter are very daring highway-robbers.

The *Thekyf*. This is a very powerful tribe, possessing the productive country about Tayf, its gardens, and other equally fertile spots on the eastern declivity of the great Hedjaz chain of mountains. Many of them are settlers. Half of the inhabitants of Tayf belong to this tribe; others of them continue to dwell in tents. Like all those mountaineers, they have few horses or camels, but are rich in flocks of sheep and goats.

The principal tribes of the Thekyf are *Beni Sofyán*, who live altogether as Bedouins; they can muster from six to seven hundred matchlocks. Two minor tribes, the *Modher* and

Rabýa, reside with the Thekyf and participate in their interests, although I doubt whether they properly belong to them. It is these Beni Rabýa, whose emigrants have peopled a considerable part of Nubia, and whose descendants are the *Kenouz* (erroneously called *Berabera* in Egypt), above the first cataract. The Thekyfs can raise two thousand matchlocks; they defended Tayf against the Wahabys.

Tribes from Tayf toward Szana in Yemen.

Of these I can only speak from report, and shall here merely notice the tribes whose territories are more particularly described in my Arabian Travels.

From Tayf along the South-eastern plain in the direction from North to South.

Proceeding eastward from Tayf, we find at Ossoma a tribe of *Ateybe*, and at Taraba, the strong tribe of *el Begoum*. From thence southward, on the back of the great chain of mountains, we find the *Beni Oklob*. At Ranye are the *Beni Sabya*, and about Wady Beishe the *Beni Sálem*, whose numbers amount to five thousand matchlocks. Southward of them are the *Beni Kahtan*, a large tribe; the strongest and most considerable between the Ateybe and Hadramaut. They possess a good breed of horses, and their camel-riders are the best soldiers of the southern plains.

The *Beni Kahtan* are subdivided into two tribes: *Es-Sahâma*—whose sheikh, *Gormola*, was very much the friend of Saoud—and the tribe of *el Aasy*, whose sheikh, Hesher, is the most renowned warrior in the whole country.

The *Beni Dowaser*, a wild tribe, but little connected with any settlers. They are great hunters of ostriches.

Of the tribes above mentioned, the Begoum, Sabya, and Beni Sálem, are partly cultivators. The Kahtan and Dowaser are exclusively Bedouins. The Kahtan are more rich in camels than any Bedouins of the Eastern Desert. A person of the middle class sometimes possesses one hundred and fifty camels, and a man is reckoned poor who has only forty. Their camels are all of a black colour.

The *Beni Kelb* are described as being half-savage.

The *Beni Yám* are cultivators in the Wády Nedjrán; a warlike tribe whom the Wahabys could not find means to subdue. Some of their members profess the Persian creed; the more orthodox among them are subdivided into the minor branches of *Okmán* and *el Marra*. There is a saying recorded of Mohammed, that " the worst of all names are Harb and Marra."

The *Beni Kholan*, bordering upon the territory of the Imám of Szana.

From Tayf along the Mountains southwards.

The *Beni Sad*. Of them and of the Kahtan Arabs (whom I mention together, as they border upon each other in a southern direction) Masowdy says, in his work entitled " The Golden Meadows," that they are the only remnants of the primitive tribes of Arabia. Most of the other tribes about Mekka,

Tayf, and Medinah, are well known in Arabian history since the propagation of Islám; others, such as Hodheyl, Koreysh, Thekyf, Fahem, Mezeyne, Harb, prior to Mohammed. But the two tribes above mentioned, the Beni Sad and Kahtan, are famous in the most remote antiquity, when Arabian history, for the greater part, is covered with complete darkness.

The *Nászera, Beni Málek, Ghámed*, and *Zohrán*. Of these three last mentioned tribes each can raise from five hundred to one thousand matchlocks; the Zohrán as many as fifteen hundred.

The *Shomrán*, a very strong tribe: these extend likewise into the eastern and western plains. The *Asábely*, the *Ibn el Ahmar*, the *Ibn el Asmar*, and *Beni Shafra*.

The *Asyr*, forming the most numerous and warlike tribe of those mountains, and exercising considerable influence over all their neighbours. They can assemble fifteen thousand men armed with matchlocks.

The *Abyde*, the *Senhán*, the *Wadaa* (a strong tribe), the *Sahhár*, and the *Bágem*.

Here begins the territory of the Imám of

Szana, and the road leads to that town through the tribes of Sofyán, Háshed, Omrán, and Hamdán.

The tribes of these mountains are all cultivators, but many individuals of them live in tents, and in spring time descend into the neighbouring plains to pasture their flocks; they possess but few horses or camels; the produce of their ground, however, is abundant, and they sell it on the coast of Yemen.

HORSES, CAMELS, AND LOCUSTS OF ARABIA.

Horses. (See Vol. I. p. 208.)

It is a general but erroneous opinion that Arabia is very rich in horses; but the breed is limited to the extent of fertile pasture grounds in that country, and it is in such parts only that horses thrive, while those Bedouins who occupy districts of poor soil rarely possess any horses. It is found, accordingly, that the tribes most rich in horses are those who dwell in the comparatively fertile plains of Mesopotamia, on the banks of the river Euphrates, and in the Syrian plains. Horses can there feed for several of the spring months upon the green grass and herbs produced by the rains in the vallies and fertile grounds, and such food seems absolutely necessary for promoting the full growth and vigour of the horse. We find that in Nedjd horses are not nearly so numerous as in the countries before mentioned, and they become scarce in proportion as we proceed towards the south.

In Hedjaz, especially in the mountainous regions of that country, and thence on towards Yemen, but few horses are to be seen, and these few are imported from the north. The Aeneze tribes on the frontiers of Syria have from eight to ten thousand horses; and some smaller tribes roving about that neighbourhood possess, probably, half as many. To the single tribe of Montefek Arabs, in the Desert watered by the river Euphrates, between Baghdad and Basrah, we may assign at least eight thousand horses, and the tribes of Dhofyr and Beni Shammar are proportionably rich in those noble quadrupeds; while the province of Nedjd, Djebel Shammar, and Kasym, (that is from the vicinity of the Persian Gulf, as far as Medinah,) do not possess above ten thousand.

Among the great tribes on the Red Sea, between Akaba and Mekka, and to the south and south-east of Mekka as far as Yemen, horses are very scarce, especially among those of the mountainous districts. In the eastern plain between Beishe and Nedjrán, horses are rather more numerous. The tribe of Kahtan, residing in that quarter, is celebrated for its excellent studs; and the same may be said of the Dowaser tribe.

The settled inhabitants of Hedjaz and Yemen are not much in the habit of keeping horses; and I believe it may be stated as a moderate and fair calculation, that between five and six thousand constitute the greatest number of horses in the country from Akaba or the north point of the Red Sea, southwards to the shores of the ocean near Hadramaut, comprising the great chain of mountains and the lower grounds on the west of it, towards the sea. The great heat of the climate in Oman is reckoned unfavourable to the breeding of horses, which are there still more scarce than in Yemen. When I affirm, therefore, that the aggregate number of horses in Arabia, (as bounded by the river Euphrates and by Syria,) does not exceed fifty thousand, (a number much inferior to what the same extent of ground in any other part of Asia or in Europe would furnish,) I am confident that my calculation is not by any means under the true estimate.

In this part of the East, I know not any country that seems to abound more in horses than Mesopotamia; the tribes of Curdes and Bedouins in that quarter probably possess greater numbers than all the Arabian Bedouins together, for the richness of the Mesopotamian pasture contributes materially to augment the breed.

The best pasturing places of Arabia not only produce the greatest number of horses, but likewise the finest and most select race. The best Koheyls of the khomse are found in Nedjd, on the Euphrates, and in the Syrian deserts; while in the southern parts of Arabia, and particularly in Yemen, no good breed exists but those which have been imported from the north. The Bedouins of Hedjaz have but few horses, their main strength consisting in camel-riders and foot-soldiers, armed with matchlocks only. In all the country from Mekka to Medinah, between the mountains and the sea, a distance of at least two hundred and sixty miles, I do not believe that two hundred horses could be found; and the same proportion of numbers may be remarked all along the Red Sea, from Yembo up to Akaba.

The united armies of all the southern Wahaby chiefs who attacked Mohammed Aly Pasha in the year 1815, at Byssel, consisting of twenty-five thousand men, had with them only five hundred horsemen, mostly belonging to Nedjd, and the followers of Faisal, one of Saoud's sons, who was present with the troops.

Both the climate and pasture of Yemen are reckoned injurious to the health of horses: many of them die from disease in that country, where they never thrive; indeed, the race begins to fall off in the very first generation. The Imám of Sana, and all the governors of Yemen, derive an annual supply of horses from Nedjd, and the inhabitants of the sea-coast receive considerable numbers by way of Sowakin from the countries bordering on the Nile. The horses taken in 1810, by the Rowalla Arabs, from the defeated troops of the Pasha of Baghdad, were all sold by them to the horse-dealers of Nedjd, and by the latter to the Arabs of Yemen; who are not, it may be here observed, by any means so nice and fastidious in choosing blood horses, as their northern neighbours. During the government of the Wahaby chief, horses became more scarce every year among his Arabs. They were sold by their owners to foreign purchasers, who took them to Yemen, Syria, and Basra; from which last-mentioned place the Indian market was supplied with Arabian horses, because they feared that Saoud or his successor might have seized them; for it had become the custom, upon any slight pretext of disobedience or unlawful conduct, to confiscate a Bedouin's mare as a forfeit to the public treasury. The possession of a mare, besides, imposed an obligation on the Bedouin of being in constant readiness to attend his chief during his wars; therefore many Arabs preferred the alternative of being altogether without horses.

In the district of Djebel Shammar, many encampments have been lately seen without a single horse, and it is well known that the Meteyr Arabs (between Medinah and Kasym, reduced the number of their horses, within a few years, from two thousand to twelve hundred. The late Sherif of Mekka possessed an excellent stud of horses: the best stallions of Nedjd were taken to Mekka for sale, and it became a fashion among the Bedouin women going on a pilgrimage to Mekka, that they should bring their husbands' stallions as presents to the Sherif, for which, however, they received in return, silk stuffs, ear-rings, and similar articles.

From all that has come to my knowledge, on the very best authority, I have no hesitation in saying, that the finest race of Arabian blood horses may be found in Syria; and that of all the Syrian districts, the most excellent in this respect is the Hauran, where the horses may be purchased at first cost, and chosen among the camps of the Arabs themselves, who occupy the plains in spring time. The horses bought up at Basra for the Indian market are purchased at second hand from Bedouin dealers, and an Arab will rarely condescend to offer a good horse at a distant market without a certainty of selling it. True blood horses of the khomse, as I have been credibly informed, seldom find their way to Basra; and most of the horses purchased there for the Indian market belong to the Montefyk Arabs, who are not very solicitous about giving a pure breed. It might perhaps be advisable for the great European powers to have persons properly qualified, employed in purchasing horses for them in Syria, as the best mode of crossing and ennobling their own studs. Damascus would be the best position for the establishment of such persons. I am induced to suspect that very few true Arabian horses, of the best breeds, and still less any of the first rate among them, have ever been imported into England, although many horses of Syria, Barbary, and Egypt, have passed under the name of Arabs.

The Bedouins are of opinion that an Egyptian mare coupled with a blood Arabian produces a good breed, much better than that of the indigenous Syrian mares, whose breed is not considered of any value, even though crossed by the Koheyl. It would be erroneous to suppose, that the horses of the khomse, or the noble breed, are all of the most perfect or distinguished quality and beauty.

Among the descendants of the famous horse Eclipse may be found mere hacks; thus I have seen many Koheyl that had little more to recommend them than their name, although the power of bearing considerable fatigue seems common to all of the Desert race. The fine horses, however, of the khomse are far more numerous than the common horses belonging to the same breed; but still, among those fine horses, there can be found only a few worthy of being entitled "first rate," in respect to size, bone, beauty, and action; perhaps not above five or six among a whole tribe. It seems a fair and probable calculation to say, that the Syrian deserts do not furnish more than two hundred of that pre-eminent description, each of which may be estimated, in the Desert itself, at from one hundred and fifty to two hundred pounds. Of these latter, I believe that very few, if any, have ever found their way to Europe, although it is through them alone that any successful attempt could be made to ennoble and improve the European race, while the horses usually exported are all of the second or third quality.

The Hedjaz Bedouins are accustomed to purchase mares from the Egyptian pilgrim caravan, and the fillies produced between these mares and good stallions they sell to the Arabs of Yemen. I never saw any geldings in the interior of the Desert.

In Egypt itself, on the borders of the Nile, there is not any breed of horses particularly distinguished. The finest of that country are produced in those districts where the best clover grows; which is in Upper Egypt, about Tahta, Akhmim, and Farshiout, and in Lower Egypt, in the territory of Menzaleh. Very few Arabian blood horses ever come to Egypt, a circumstance not surprising, since their remarkable quality, the power of supporting fatigue, is but little requisite on the fertile borders of the Nile.

The Egyptian horse is ugly and of a coarse make, resembling more a coach horse than a racer. His chief defects are, clumsy legs and knees, a short and thick neck. The head is sometimes fine; but I never saw an Egyptian horse having handsome legs.

They are not able to bear any considerable fatigue; but those that are well fed display much more brilliant action than the Arabian horses: their impetuosity renders them particularly desirable for heavy cavalry, and it is from this quality of the horse that the Egyptian cavalry have always founded their claim to celebrity. In their first onset the Egyptian horses are much superior to the Arabian; but when long marches become necessary, and the duties of light cavalry required, the Egyptians prove themselves infinitely less useful than the Koheyl.

The Libyan Bedouins derive their supplies of horses from their own breeds, as well as from Egypt. In the interior of the Desert, and towards Barbary, they are said to have preserved the ancient breeds of Arabian horses; but this is not the case in the vicinity of Egypt, where the peculiar races are as little distinguished as among the Egyptians. Like the Arabian Bedouins, those Libyans exclusively ride mares.

Respecting the pedigrees of Arabian horses I must here add, that in the interior of the Desert the Bedouins never refer to any among themselves; for they as well know the whole genealogy of their horses, as they do that of the owners. But when they take their horses to market at any town, such as Basra, Baghdad, Aleppo, Damascus, Medinah, or Mekka, they carry along with them a written pedigree, which they present to the purchaser; and it is only on such occasions that a Bedouin is ever found to possess the written pedigree of his horse; while, on the other hand, in the interior of the Desert itself, he would laugh at being asked for the pedigree of his mare. This may serve to correct an erroneous account, elsewhere given, on the subject of such pedigrees.

In Upper Egypt the Maazy and Heteym Arabs, occupying the Desert between the Nile and the Red Sea, have preserved among them the breed of the khomse. As in Arabia, horses are possessed by them in partnership. They divide each horse into twenty-four shares, or *kerat* (according to the division of landed property in Egypt, which is always by kerats), and different persons buy three, four, or eight kerats of the mare, and share proportionably in the benefits arising from the sale of the young breed. So little is known concerning the true breed of horses among the soldiers in Egypt, that when in the year 1812 Ibrahim Pasha's troops took ten Koheyl horses belonging to Heteym, the soldiers sold them one to another, as if they had been common Egyptian horses; while their former possessors valued them at least three times beyond that amount.

For a hundred Spanish dollars a good cavalry horse may, at any time, be purchased in Egypt. The highest price paid for an Egyptian horse is three hundred dollars; but for this horse a Bedouin would not give fifty dollars. The Mamelouks formerly esteemed the Koheyl of the Desert, and expended considerable sums in propagating their breed in Egypt. The present masters of this country have not the same passion for fine horses as their predecessors; who, in many respects, had adopted Arab notions, and had made it a fashion among them to acquire a competent knowledge of horses, and to keep their stables upon a most extravagant establishment.

Here may be added to the names of Arabian breeds already mentioned :—

El Thámerye, of the Koheyl race.

El Nezahhy, a breed of the *Hadaba.* Some tribes reckon the Nezakhy stallions among the number of blood horses.

The *Manekye* and *Djolfe* are not considered as belonging to the khomse by the Arabs of Nedjd.

The Hadaba and Dahma breeds are much esteemed in Nedjd.

The horses of the Mesenna breed (of the Koheyl race) are never used in Nedjd as stallions.

The Bedouins use all the horses of the khomse exclusively as stallions. The first horse produced by a mare belonging to a race not comprehended within the khomse, would, notwithstanding its beauty, and perhaps superior qualities, never be employed as a breeder. The favourite mare of Saoud, the Wahaby chief, which he constantly rode on his expeditions, and whose name, *Keraye,* became famous all over Arabia, brought forth a horse of uncommon beauty and excellence. The mare, however, not being of the khomse, Saoud would not permit his people to use that fine horse as a stallion ; and not knowing what to do with it, as Bedouins never ride horses, he sent it as a present to the Sherif. The mare, Keraye, had been purchased by Saoud from a Bedouin of the Kahtan Arabs for fifteen hundred dollars.

A troop of Druses on horseback attacked, in the summer of 1815, a party of Bedouins in Hauran, and drove them into their encampment, where they were in turn assailed by a superior force, and all killed except one man, who fled. He was pursued by several of the best mounted Bedouins; but his mare, although fatigued, continued her speed for several hours, and could not be overtaken. Before his pursuers gave up the chase they cried out to him, promising quarter and safe conduct, and begging that he would allow them to kiss the forehead of his excellent mare. Upon his refusal, they desisted from pursuing, and, blessing the generous creature, they exclaimed, addressing her owner, "Go and wash the feet of your mare, and drink up the water." This expression is used by the Bedouins to show their great love for such mares, and their sense of the services which they have rendered.

The Bedouins in general do not allow their

mares to breed until they have completed their fifth year; but the poorer classes, who are eager for the profits arising from the sale of foals, sometimes wait no longer than the completion of the fourth year.

The price paid in Nedjd, when a stallion is occasionally hired, merely for the purpose of breeding, is one Spanish dollar; but the owner of the horse is entitled to decline the acceptance of this dollar as payment: if he think fit, he may wait until the mare brings forth. Should she produce a filly, he may claim a she-camel of one year; if the offspring prove male, he takes, in like manner, a young he-camel, as payment for the use of his stallion.

The Bedouins never allow a horse, at the moment of its birth, to fall upon the ground: they receive it in their arms, and so cherish it for several hours, occupied in washing and stretching its tender limbs, and caressing it as they would a baby. After this they place it on the ground, and watch its feeble steps with particular attention, prognosticating from that time the excellencies or defects of their future companion.

In Nedjd, the people feed their horses regularly upon dates. At Derayeh, and in the country of El Hassa, dates are mixed with the *birsim*, or dried clover, and given to them as food. Barley, however, is the most usual provender throughout all parts of Arabia. The wealthy inhabitants of Nedjd frequently give flesh to their horses, raw as well as boiled, together with all the fragments of their own meals. I know a man at Hamah, in Syria, who assured me that he had often given to his horses roasted meat before the commencement of a fatiguing journey, that they might be the better able to endure it. The same person also related to me, that fearing lest the governor of the town should take a liking to his favorite horse, he fed it for a fortnight exclusively upon roasted pork, which excited its spirit and mettle to such a height, that it became absolutely unmanageable, and could be no longer an object of desire to the governor.

I have seen vicious horses in Egypt cured of the habit of biting, by presenting to them, while in the act of doing so, a leg of mutton just taken from the fire: the pain which a horse feels in biting through the hot meat causes it, after a few lessons, to abandon the vicious habit. Egyptian horses are much less gentle in their temper than the Arabian; they are often vicious—the Arabians scarcely ever—and require to be constantly tied, while the Arab horses wander freely and quietly about the camps like camels. Egyptian grooms are celebrated all over the East for their treatment of horses; insomuch that the Pashas and grandees throughout Asiatic Turkey make it a rule to have always a couple of them in their service They curry the horse three or four times a day, and devote so much of their time and trouble to it, that it is usual in all parts of Egypt to have as many grooms as horses in the stable, each groom having the peculiar charge of one horse only.

The Wahaby chief, who possesses, indisputably, the finest stud of horses in the whole East, never allows his mares to be mounted until they have completed their fourth year. The common Bedouins, however, frequently ride them even before they have attained their third year.

It has been forbidden by the Wahaby chief, that his Arabs should sell one third of a mare, as frequently is practised by the Northern Aenezes. He alleges, that this custom often leads to unlawful and cheating tricks; but he permits the selling of one half of the mare. (See the preceding remarks on horses, Vol. I. p. 203.)

Camels.—(See Vol. I. p. 194.)

Between the races of camels in the northern and southern countries, there is a considerable difference. In Syria and Mesopotamia they are covered by thick hair, and in general attain to a much greater size than in Hedjaz, where they have very little wool. The Nubian camel has short hair like a deer, as likewise the Nubian sheep which prevents the Bedouins of that country from living under tents, (fabricated in Arabia from goat's and camel's hair), they are therefore obliged to construct portable huts made of mats and reeds; the Arabian camels are generally brown: many black camels are seen also among them. The further we approach the south in Egypt, the lighter becomes the colour. Towards Nubia the camels are mostly white, and I never saw a black one in that country.

The largest camels are those from Anadolia, of the Turkman breed: the smallest that I have seen are those from Yemen. In the Eastern Desert the camels reputed best for carriage, are those of the Beni Tay, in Mesopotamia, near the river Euphrates. In mountainous countries camels are certainly scarce; but it is an erroneous opinion to think that camels are not capable of ascending hills. Thus in Hedjaz their numbers are very limited, because pasture is scanty. The country most rich and abundant in camels, is undoubtedly Nedjd, entitled on that account *Om el Bel,* or "The mother of camels." It furnishes Syria, Hedjaz, and Yemen with camels, which in those countries are worth double the price paid originally for them in Nedjd. During my residence in Hedjaz, a good camel was there estimated at the price of sixty dollars; and such was the want of pasturage and scarcity of provisions, that within three years, upon a moderate calculation, there died thirty thousand camels belonging to the Pasha of Egypt, at that time commanding in Hedjaz.

The Turkmans and Kurds from Anadolia purchase, every year, eight or ten thousand camels in the Syrian deserts, of which the greater number are brought there by dealers from Nedjd. They use them in propagating the breed of Turkman camels called *Maya* (see the former account).

No country in the East is so remarkable for the rapid propagation of camels as Nedjd, during years of fertility. The Nedjd camels are likewise less susceptible of epidemic diseases (and especially the *Djam*, which is much dreaded in various quarters of the Desert,) than any others; and on that account principally they are preferred by the Bedouins, who from the most distant parts of Arabia repair to Nedjd that they may renew their flocks.

Among the Bedouins, female camels are always more esteemed and dearer than the males. In Syria and Egypt, on the contrary, where the camels are chiefly wanted for their strength in bearing heavy loads, the males are most valued. The people who inhabit the towns and villages of Nedjd ride only she-camels on their journies, because these support thirst better than the males; but the Bedouins generally prefer he-camels for riding. The common load of an Arabian camel is from four to five hundred pounds upon a short journey, and from three to four hundred pounds on a journey of considerable distance. The camels employed between Djidda and Tayf in the year 1814, or 1815, for carrying provisions to Mohammed Aly, had loads not exceeding two hundred and fifty pounds. The well-fed and well-watered Egyptian camels are equal in strength to the Anadolian; those of the largest size at Cairo will carry three bales of coffee, or fifteen hundred weight, from the town to the water side, about three miles distant. From Cairo to Suez, the same camels will carry ten hundred weight; and that space is a journey of three days. The longer the journey to be undertaken, and the fewer wells to be found on the way, the lighter are the loads. The Darfur camels are distinguished for their size and great strength in bearing fatigue under heavy loads; in this latter quality they surpass all the camels of North-Eastern Africa. Those which accompany the Darfur caravan to Egypt, are seldom loaded with more than four quintals. The Sennár camels generally carry three and a half, and are not equal in size to those of Darfur.

The capability of bearing thirst varies considerably among the different races of camels. The Anadolian, accustomed to cold climates, and countries copiously watered on all sides, must, every second day, have its supply of water; and if this be withheld in summer-time until the third day, on a journey, the camel often sinks under the privation. During the winter, in Syrian latitudes and in the Northern Arabian Desert, camels very seldom drink unless when on a journey; the first succulent herbs sufficiently moisten their stomachs at that season of the year. In summer-time the Nedjd camel must be watered on the evening of every fourth day; a longer exposure to thirst on a journey would probably be fatal to him.

I believe that all over Arabia four whole days constitute the utmost extent to which camels can stretch their capability of enduing thirst in summer; nor is it necessary that they should be compelled to thirst longer, for there is no territory in the route of any traveller crossing Arabia where wells are farther distant than a journey of three entire days, or three and a half. In case of absolute necessity, an Arabian camel might perhaps go five days without drinking, but the traveller must never reckon upon such an extraordinary circumstance; and after the camel has gone three whole days without water, it shows manifest signs of great distress.

The indigenous Egyptian camels are less qualified to endure fatigue than any others that I know: being from their birth well watered and fed on the fertile banks of the river Nile, they are but little accustomed to journies in the Desert of any considerable length; and during the pilgrims' march to Mekka, several of them daily perish. There are not, of any race, camels that bear thirst more patiently than those of Darfur. The caravans coming from that country to Egypt, must travel nine or ten days' journies on a route which does not furnish any water; and over this extent of ground they often pass during the heats of summer. It is true that many of the camels die upon the road, and no merchant undertakes such an expedition without a couple of spare camels in reserve; but the greater number reach Egypt. There is not the slightest probability that an Arabian camel could ever perform such a journey, and still less a Syrian or Egyptian. The camels in most parts of Africa are more hardy than the Arabian.

Although I have often heard anecdotes related of Arabs, who on their long journies were frequently reduced to the utmost distress by want of water, yet I never understood that a camel had been slaughtered for the sake of finding a supply in its stomach. Without absolutely denying the possibility of such a circumstance, I do not hesitate to affirm that it can have occurred but very seldom; indeed the last stage of thirst renders a traveller so unwilling and unable to support the exertion of walking, that he continues his journey on the back of his camel in hopes of finding water, rather than expose himself to certain destruction by killing the serviceable creature. I have frequently seen camels slaughtered, but never discovered in the stomachs of any, except those which had been watered on the same day, a copious supply of water. The Darfur caravans are often reduced to incredible suffering by want of water; yet they never have resort to the expedient above mentioned. It may perhaps be practised in other parts of Africa, but it seems unknown in Arabia; nor have I ever heard, either in Arabia or Nubia, that camel's urine mixed with water was used to allay the creature's thirst in cases of extreme distress.

What is called in Egypt and Africa *hedjein*, and in Arabia *deloul*, (both terms signifying the camels trained for riding,) is in fact the same race with the heavy carrying beast, distinguished from the latter only as a hunter is from a coach-horse. Whenever an Arab perceives in one of his young camels any indication of its being small and extremely active, he trains it for the purposes of riding; and if it be a female, he takes care to match her with a fine well-bred male. For the temporary use of a male camel on such occasions the price is one dollar, among the Arabian Bedouins; being the same price that is paid for the similar services of a hired stallion. The breeds which I have mentioned are those of heavy transport camels, as well as the lighter kind destined for the saddle.

In Arabia, the best camels for riding, those of the most swift and easy trot, are said to be in the province of *Oman*. The *deloul el Omány*, is celebrated in all the songs of the Arabs. While I was at Djidda, Mohammed Aly Pasha received two of those camels as a present from the Imám of Maskat; they were sent by sea. In their appearance it would not perhaps have been easy to distinguish them from other Arabian camels; their legs, however, were somewhat more straight and slender; but there was in their eyes a noble expression, and something in the whole deportment, by which, among all animals, the generous may be distinguished from the common breed. Of other *delouls* in Arabia, the breeds most esteemed are those belonging to the tribes of Howeytat, of Sebaa (an Aeneze family), and of Sherarat. In North-Eastern Africa, where the deloul is called *hedjein*, the Sennár breed and that of the Nubian Bedouins are much preferred to any others for riding. The Darfur camels are by much too heavy to be used as hedjeins for the purposes of saddle-riding.

The good Nubian hedjeins are so very docile, and have so swift and pleasant an amble, that they supply the want of horses better than any other camels; most of them are whitish. In swiftness they surpass any of the various camels that I have seen throughout those parts of the East.

The name of *oshàry* (implying a camel that travels in one day a ten days' journey) is known in Egypt and Nubia, where incredible stories are related concerning a race of camels that were accustomed to perform very wonderful expeditions. I have reason to doubt whether they ever existed but in the imagination of fanciful Bedouins. Were I to repeat the tales of Arabian and Nubian Bedouins on this subject, the circumstances would appear similar to those which too credulous travellers report of the Barbary camels, or a particular breed of them; circumstances which I shall never believe until they can be ascertained beyond doubt, and proved to be facts. An Ababde Bedouin told me once, at Assouan, that his grandfather went on some occasion from that place in one day to Siout, a journey of at least two hundred and fifty miles; and that the camel which had performed such an expedition, was not in the slightest degree fatigued. But I never could positively ascertain an instance of greater swiftness than what I shall immediately mention, and am persuaded that very few camels in Egypt or Nubia are capable of such an exertion.

The greatest performance of a hedjein that ever came to my knowledge, satisfactorily ascertained on credible authority, is that of a camel belonging to a Mamelouk Bey of Esne, in Upper Egypt, which he had purchased from a Bisharein chief for one hundred and fifty Spanish dollars. This camel was to go for a wager, in one day between sun-rise and sun-set, from Esne to Genne and back again, the whole distance being equal to a space of one hundred and thirty miles. It arrived about four o'clock in the afternoon at a village sixteen miles distant from Esne, where its strength failed, after having travelled about one hundred and fifteen miles in eleven hours, and twice passed over the Nile in a ferry-boat; this passage across the river requiring at least twenty minutes. A good English trotting mare could do the same, or perhaps more, but probably not in such a warm climate as that of Egypt. Without so much forced exertion, that camel would probably have gone a distance of one hundred and eighty or even two hundred miles within the space of twenty-four hours; which, according to the slow rate of caravan-travelling, might be reckoned as equivalent to ten days' journies; therefore, the boast above mentioned, of performing a journey of ten days in one day may not appear altogether extravagant.

But it would be absurd to suppose any beast capable of running ten times, for an entire day, as a man could go on foot during the same space of time; and the swiftness of a camel never approaches, for short distances, even to that of a common horse. The gallop of a camel (which is not that quadruped's natural pace) it can never sustain above half an hour, and its forced exertion in galloping never produces a degree of speed equal to that of an ordinary horse. The forced trot of a camel is not so contrary to his nature, and he will support it for several hours without evincing many symptoms of being distressed. But even of that forced trot I must here remark, that it is much less expeditious than the same pace of a moderately good horse, and I believe that the rate of twelve miles an hour is the utmost degree of celerity in trotting that the very best hedjein can accomplish; it may perhaps gallop at fullest speed eight or even nine miles in half an hour, but it cannot support so violent an exertion for any longer time.

It is not, therefore, by extreme celerity that the hedjeins or delouls are distinguished, however surprising may be the stories related on that subject, both in Europe and in the East. But they are perhaps unequalled by any quadrupeds for the ease with which they carry their rider during an uninterrupted journey of several days and nights, when they are allowed to persevere in their own favourite pace, which is a kind of gentle and easy amble, at the rate of about five miles or five miles and a half in the hour. To describe this pleasant ambling pace, the Arabs say of a good deloul, " His back is so soft that you may drink a cup of coffee while you ride upon him." At the rate above mentioned, if properly fed every evening (or in case of emergency only once in two days), the strong camel will continue ambling for five or six days. I know of camels that went from Baghdad to Sokhne (in the Desert of Aleppo) within the space of five days. This is a caravan journey of twenty-one days. Messengers sometimes arrive at Aleppo on the seventh day after they have left Baghdad, distant a journey of twenty-five days, according to the common calculation; and I have known couriers go from Cairo by land to Mekka (forty-five days' usual journies) in eighteen days, without even changing their camels.

VOL. II.

The first thing about which an Arab is solicitous respecting his camel, when going to undertake a long journey, is the hump. Should he find this well furnished with fat, the Arab knows that his camel will endure considerable fatigue even with a very moderate allowance of food, because he believes that, according to the Arabic saying, "The camel, during the time of that expedition, will feed upon the fat of its own hump." The fact is, that as soon as the hump subsides, the camel begins to desist from much exertion, and gradually yields to fatigue. After a long journey the creature almost loses the hump, and it requires three or four months of repose and copious nourishment to restore it; which, however, does not take place until long after the other parts of the body have been replenished with flesh. Few animals exhibit so rapid a conversion of food into fat, as camels. A few days' rest and plentiful nourishment produce a visible augmentation of flesh, while, on the contrary, a few days employed in travelling without food reduce the creature almost immediately to little more than a skeleton, excepting the hump, which resists the effects of fatigue and starvation much longer.

If a camel has reached the full degree of fatness, his hump assumes the shape of a pyramid, extending its base over the entire back, and occupying altogether one fourth of the creature's whole body. But none of this description are ever seen in cultivated districts, where camels are always, more or less, obliged to work. They are only found among the wealthy Bedouins in the interior of the Desert, who keep whole herds of camels merely for the purpose of propagating the breed, and seldom force more than a few of the herd to labour. In spring time, their camels, having been fed for a couple of months upon the tender verdure, increase so much in fat, that they no longer seem belonging to that species of the hard-labouring, caravan or peasant camel.

After the fore teeth of the camel have reached their full length, the first pair of back teeth appear in the beginning of the sixth year; but two years more must elapse before they attain their greatest size. Early in the eighth year the second pair of back teeth, standing behind, and quite separate from the other teeth, make their appearance; and when they are complete, in the tenth year, the third and last pair push forward, and, like the former, grow for two years. The camel, therefore, has not completed its full growth before the twelfth year, and then it is called *rás*. To know the age of a camel under that period, the back teeth are always inspected. The camel lives as long as forty years; but after twenty-five or thirty his activity begins to fail, and he is no longer capable of enduring much fatigue. If a camel that has passed his sixteenth year become lean, the Arabs say that he can never be again rendered fat; and in that case they generally sell him at a low price to the peasants, who feed their cattle better than the inhabitants of the Desert.

The common hedjein saddle in Egypt (very slightly differing from a horse-saddle) is called *ghabeit*. The hedjein saddle of the Nubians, imported likewise into Egypt, and very neatly worked in leather, is called *gissa*. The pack-saddle of the Egyptian peasant, different from that of the Arabians and Syrians, is called *shaghour.* (From this word the Arabians derive an opprobrious appellation, which they bestow upon the Egyptian peasants, whom they style *shaghaore.*) The pack-saddles of the Libyan, Nubian, and Upper Egyptian Bedouins are called *Hawýe*, and are the same as those of the Arabians.

The deloul saddle is, throughout every part of Arabia, called *shedád*. The asses in Hedjaz are saddled with the *shedád*, differing only in proportionable size from that used with the deloul.

In Hedjaz the name of *shebrýe* is given to a kind of palanquin, having a seat made of twisted straw, about five feet in length, which is placed across the saddle of the camel, with ropes fastened to it. On its four sides are slender poles, joined above by cross bars, over which either mats or carpets are placed, to shade the traveller from the sun. This among the natives of Hedjaz is the favourite vehicle for travelling, because it admits of their stretching themselves at full length, and sleeping at pleasure.

Similar machines of the palanquin kind, but on a shorter and narrower scale, are placed lengthways on both sides of the camel's saddle, and then called *shekdef*. One person sits in each of them, but they do not allow of his stretching out at full length. Both of these shekdefs are covered, likewise, with carpets thrown across; and this vehicle is principally used for the conveyance of women.

Different from that is the *taht roán* (or rather *takht ravàn*, as the Persians, from whom the term is borrowed, call it); a litter carried by two camels, one before, and the other behind. In this kind of vehicle the great pilgrims travel: but it is more frequently used by the Turks than by the Arabians.

It is the fashion in Egypt to shear the hedjein as closely as a sheep is shorn; and this is done merely from a notion that it improves the beast's appearance. The French, during their occupation of Egypt, had established a corps of about five hundred camel-riders, whom they selected from the number of their most brave and excellent soldiers, and by means of whom they succeeded in checking the Bedouins. Many horsemen among the troops of the Pasha of Egypt have been ordered by him to keep hedjeins; and his son, Ibrahim Pasha, has about two hundred of his men mounted in that manner.

The hedjeins of Egypt are guided by a string attached to a nose-ring. Those of Arabia are very seldom perforated in the nose; and are more obedient to the short stick of the rider than to the bridle.

The Arab women, on all occasions, make a great display in the fitting-out of their camel-saddle. A woman of Nedjd would think herself degraded, were she to ride upon any other than a black camel; but, on the contrary, a lady of the Aenezes much prefers a grey or white camel.

The practice of mounting upon camels small swivel-guns, which turn upon the pommel of the saddle, is not known in Egypt. I have seen them in Syria; and they appear to be common in Mesopotamia and Baghdad. Although of little real service, yet against Arabs these small swivel-guns are a very excellent and appropriate weapon, more adapted to inspire them with terror than the heaviest pieces of artillery.

The price of a camel is found to vary in

almost every place: thus, in Egypt, according to the abundance and cheapness of provisions, the price of the same camel may fluctuate from twelve to forty dollars. A good dromedary, or hedjein, from Nubia, sometimes will cost at Cairo eighty dollars. In Hedjaz very high prices are paid for camels; fifty and sixty dollars are sometimes given for a deloul of the most common kind. There is a considerable demand in Nedjd for delouls of the first quality. Saoud has been known to pay as much as three hundred dollars for an Omán camel.

The Arabs distinguish in their camels va- that very much affect their value. The principal defect is called *el asaab*: this is in the camel's fetlock; and they regard it as incurable, and a proof of great weakness. The next is *el fekeh,* a strong tremor in the hind legs of the camel when it couches down, or rises up: this, likewise, is considered as a proof of weakness. *El serrar,* ulcerations below the chest; *el hellel, el fahoura,* and many others. Most of the caravan camels are broken-winded (or *sedreh khorbán*) from excessive fatigue, and the carrying of too heavy loads. When this circumstance occurs, the Arabs cauterise the camel's chest. They resort also to the same process, cautery, in cases of wounds on the camel's hump, and of injuries frequently occasioned by bad pack-saddles, and burdens of too great weight. Towards the close of a long journey scarcely any evening passes without the cauterising operation, yet the next morning the load is placed again upon the part so recently burnt: but no degree of pain induces the generous camel to refuse the load, or throw it on the ground. It cannot, however, be forced to rise, if from hunger or excessive fatigue its strength has failed.

Locusts.

It has been remarked in my different journals, that these destructive creatures are found in Egypt, all along the river Nile as far as Sennar, in the Nubian, and in all parts of the Arabian deserts. Those that I have seen in Upper Egypt came all from the north; those that I saw in Nubia were all said to have come from Upper Egypt. It seems, therefore, that such parts of Africa are not the native places of the locusts. In the year 1813, they devoured the whole harvest from Berber to Shendy in the Black countries; and in the spring of that same year I had seen whole flights of them in Upper Egypt, where they are particularly injurious to the palm-trees. These they strip of every leaf and green particle, the trees remaining like skeletons with bare branches.

In Arabia the locusts are known to come invariably from the East, and the Arabs accordingly say that they are produced by the ~~waters of the Persian~~ Gulf. The province of Nedjd is particularly exposed to their ravages; they overwhelm it sometimes to such a degree, that having destroyed the harvest they penetrate by thousands into the private dwellings, and devour whatever they can find, even the leather of the water vessels. It has been observed, that those locusts which come from the East are not considered so formidable, because they only fix upon trees, and do not destroy the seed; but they soon give birth to a new brood, and it is the young locusts, before they are sufficiently grown to fly away, that consume the crops. According to general report, the locusts breed as often as three times in the year.

The Bedouins who occupy the peninsula of Sinai are frequently driven to despair by the multitudes of locusts, which constitute a land plague, and a most serious grievance. These animals arrive by way of Akaba (therefore from the East), towards the end of May, when the Pleiades are setting, according to observations made by the Arabs, who believe that the locusts entertain a considerable dread of that constellation. They remain there generally during a space of forty or fifty days, and then disappear for the rest of the year.

Some few are seen in the course of every year, but great flights every fourth or fifth year; such is the general course of their unwelcome visits. Since the year 1811, however, they have invaded the peninsula every successive season for five years, in considerable numbers.

All the Bedouins of Arabia, and the inhabitants of towns in Nedjd and Hedjaz, are accustomed to eat the locusts. I have seen at Medinah and Tayf locust-shops, where these animals were sold by measure. In Egypt and Nubia they are only eaten by the poorest beggars. The Arabs, in preparing locusts as an article of food, throw them alive into boiling water, with which a good deal of salt has been mixed; after a few minutes they are taken out, and dried in the sun; the head, feet, and wings are then torn off, the bodies are cleansed from the salt and perfectly dried; after which process whole sacks are filled with them by the Bedouins. They are sometimes eaten broiled in butter; and they often contribute materials for a breakfast, when spread over unleavened bread mixed with butter.

It may here seem worthy of remark, that among all the Bedouins with whom I have been acquainted in Arabia, those of Sinai alone do not use the locusts as an article of food.

MATERIALS

FOR A HISTORY OF

THE WAHÁBYS.

MATERIALS

FOR A HISTORY OF

THE WAHÁBYS.

INTRODUCTION.

Respecting the Wahábys, various contradictory and erroneous statements have been given in the few accounts hitherto published. Some anecdotes of those remarkable sectaries, collected from the best sources of information to which I could obtain access in the East, may prove interesting to many readers. I must, however, regret, that during my residence in Hedjáz this country was, on account of the war with Mohammed Aly, closed against the people of Nedjd, who, above all others, were qualified to give faithful and accurate details of the Wahábys; while those Bedouins of the common classes, who had adopted the new faith, were, in general, wholly ignorant of its true import and doctrines.

The religion and government of the Waházbys may be very briefly defined, as a Muselmán puritanism, and a Bedouin government, in which the great chief is both the political and religious leader of the nation, exercising his authority in the same manner as the followers of Mohammed did over his converted countrymen. The founder of this sect is already known: a learned Arabian, named *Abd el Waháb*, who had visited various schools of the principal cities in the East (as is much the practice with his countrymen even now), being convinced by what he had observed during his travels, that the primitive faith of *Islám*, or Mohammedism, had become totally corrupted, and obscured by abuses, and that the far greater part of the people of the East, and especially the Turks, might be justly regarded as heretics.

But new doctrines and opinions are as little acceptable in the East as they are in the West; and no attention was paid to *Abd el Waháb* until, after long wanderings in Arabia, he retired with his family to Derayeh, at the period when Mohammed Ibn Saoud was the principal person of the town. This man became his first convert, and soon after married his daughter. These two families, therefore, must not be mistaken for each other. Abd el Waháb, the founder of the sect, was, by birth, of the tribe of *Temym*, and of the clan called El Wahábe. The Beni Temym are, for the greater part, husbandmen in Nedjd; their principal place of abode is at El Howta, a village five days' journey from Derayeh, southerly, in the direction of Wady Dowasyr, and the birth-place of Abd el Waháb. Another colony of the Temym inhabit the town of *Keffár*, in the province of Djebel Shammar, and are the descendants of families who fled from Howta, in order to escape the consequences of the blood-revenge. A third colony are husbandmen, under the jurisdiction of the Pasha of Baghdad, in the villages between Helle and Meshed Aly.

The Beni Temym are noted for their lofty stature, broad heads, and thick beards; characteristics which distinguish them from other Bedouins.

But the family of Saoud, the political founder of the Waháby government, is of the tribe of *Messálykh*, a branch of the Wold Aly, and therefore belonging to the Aeneze. The clan of the Messálykh, called Mokren (مُكرن) or, as the Bedouins also pronounce it, *Medjren*, to which Saoud belonged, had settled at Derayeh, and acquired influence there; and it was to them that Abd el Waháb addressed himself. Mohammed Ibn Saoud was the first who assumed the title of *Emír;* but his force was then so small, that in his first skirmish with some enemies, as it is related, he had only seven camel-riders with him.

To trace the history of this sect, is to record facts similar to those which are daily occurring in the Desert. A tribe is fortunate, rises into power, takes booty, and extends its influence over its neighbours. By unwearied exertions and efforts, Abd el Azyz and Ibn Saoud, the son and grandson of the first leader, Mohammed, succeeded in carrying their arms to the remotest corners of Arabia ; and while they propagated their religious tenets, they established a supremacy of power conformably with these tenets, which taught the Arabs to acknowledge a spiritual and temporal leader in the same person, as they had done on the first promulgation of Islám. I shall resume their history, though I am unable to give with accuracy very few dates prior to the campaign of Mohammed Aly. But it seems necessary to begin by explaining the principles upon which the religion and government were founded.

The doctrines of Abd el Waháb were not those of a new religion ; his efforts were directed only to reform abuses in the followers of Islám, and to disseminate the pure faith among Bedouins ; who, although nominally Muselmáns, were equally ignorant of religion, as indifferent about all the duties which it prescribed. As generally has been the case with reformers, he was misunderstood both by his friends and his enemies. The latter, hearing of a new sect, which accused the Turks of heresy, and held their prophet, Mohammed, in much less veneration than they did, were easily persuaded that a new creed was professed, and that the Wahábys were consequently not merely heretics, but *káfirs*, or infidels. They were the more confirmed in this belief, first, by the artifices of the Sherif Gháleb of Mekka, and secondly, by the alarm raised among all the neighbouring Pashas. The Sherif of Mekka, who had always been a determined enemy of the growing Waháby power, had an interest in widening the breach between the new sectaries and the Turkish empire, and therefore artfully and unremittingly spread reports of the Wahábys being really infidels, in order to render abortive all attempts at negotiation with them. The Pashas of Baghdad, Damascus, and Cairo, who were nearest to the dreaded Bedouins, were no less eager in representing under the blackest colours, the designs of these enemies of the Turkish abuses, and as they consequently inferred, of the Turkish faith. They had either to conduct, or to send an escort with the pilgrim caravans to the holy cities, and it became their interest to magnify the dangers on the road, in order to be excused if any accident should befall the caravan, or to be justified in keeping it back, which they secretly wished to do, as the departure of the caravans subjects all these Pashas to very great expenses. Added to this, were the reports of many hadjys or pilgrims who had gone by sea to Djidda and Mekka, and had suffered from the insolence of the Waháby soldiers, and in some instances were not permitted to perform the pilgrimage. Upon their return, they exaggerated their sufferings, and a description of the Wahábys could not, certainly, be given by them with impartiality. We need not, therefore, be surprised if it became generally believed throughout the East, that the Wahábys were endeavouring to establish an entirely new religion, and that they treated all Turks with increased cruelty because they were Muselmáns — a belief which the conduct of the great body of the Wahábys themselves was not calculated to invalidate. These were Bedouins who, before they knew Wahábyism, had been almost wholly ignorant of Islám, and whose notions of it now were very imperfect. The new doctrines were therefore likely to appear to them as a new religion, and especially so, when they learned the different customs and tenets of the Turkish hadjys, and the Arabian inhabitants of towns, and compared them with their own. The spirit of fanaticism which their chief fostered by all the means in his power, did not permit them to draw nice distinctions in a matter about which they had themselves very imperfect notions; and this satisfactorily explains, how it happened that they accused the Turks of being infidels, and were in their turn treated by the latter as such. The few intelligent Syrians or Egyptians, who, having been on the pilgrimage, had found opportunities to converse with the well-informed sectaries, might probably be convinced that the Bedouin creed was that of Islam; and although the opinions of both parties might not agree in all points, yet they felt the injustice of calling the Wahábys infidels. But the testimony of such persons, if they ever dared to give it, without exposing themselves to the charge of being bad Muselmáns, was unavailing in the general outcry; and especially after the year 1803, when the hadj caravans were finally interrupted, an opinion prevailed generally, that the Wahabys were determined enemies of the Muselmán religion. In two short treatises on the Wahabys, written at Baghdad and Aleppo, about 1808,* by M. Rousseau, it is positively asserted, that the Wahabys have a new religion, and that although they acknowledge the Koran, yet they have entirely abolished the pilgrimage to Mekka. This was certainly the vulgar opinion about that time at Aleppo; but more accurate information might have easily been obtained from intelligent pilgrims and Bedouins even in that town; and it is surprising that it should not, as the author was professedly giving a description of the Wahábys, and as he states that he derived part of his information "du Chapelain de Saoud," implying an office in the court of Derayeh, respecting the nature of which I am not able to form any exact notion.

Since the army of Mohammed Aly established itself in Hedjaz, and the intrigues

* The first is the "Description of the Pashalick of Baghdad," the other a Memoir in the "Mines de l'Orient."

of Sherif Gháleb became no longer of any avail, direct communications too having been opened with the Waháby chiefs as well as with the inferior leaders, and the pilgrim-caravans having resumed their ancient route, the real character of the Wahábys is better known, even in the distant parts of the Turkish dominions; and the gratitude which the people of Mekka express towards their temporary masters, is likely to impress with the most favourable ideas, every pilgrim who there inquires after the new sect.

If farther proof were required that the Wahabys are very orthodox Muselmáns, their catechism would furnish it. When Saoud took possession of Mekka, he distributed copies of this catechism among the inhabitants, and ordered that the pupils in public schools should learn it by heart. Its contents are nothing more than what the most orthodox Turk must admit to be true. Saoud entertained an absurd notion, that the town's-people were brought up in entire ignorance of their religion, and therefore wished to instruct those of Mekka in its first principles. Nothing, however, was contained in this catechism which the Mekkans had not already learned; and when Saoud found that they were better informed than his own people, he desisted from further disseminating it among them.

The chief doctrines of the Wahabys, it will be seen, correspond with those taught in other parts of the Muselman empire. The Koran and the traditions of Mohammed (*Sunne*) are acknowledged as fundamental, comprising the laws; and the opinions of the best commentators on the Koran are respected, although not implicitly followed. In the attempt, however, to exhibit the primitive practices and pure dogmas of the original founder of Islám and of his first followers, as established upon these laws, they were naturally led to condemn a number of false opinions and corruptions which had crept into Islám as at this day taught, and also to point out the numerous cases in which Turks acted in direct opposition to the precepts they themselves acknowledged to be indispensable. I am not qualified by a sufficient knowledge of the controversy, to present my reader with full details on this head, and shall therefore confine myself to the notice of a few instances, which are considered as the chief points of dispute between the two parties: the Wahábys reproach the Turks with honouring the prophet, in a manner which approaches adoration, and with doing the same also to the memory of many saints. In this they seem not to be much mistaken. By once admitting the Koran as their revealed law, the Turks were obliged to believe implicitly the numerous passages wherein it is expressly declared that Mohammed is a mortal like themselves: but the fanatic love for their prophet could not be content with this modest declaration; their learned men proved with sophistical subtlety that the prophet, although dead and buried, had not shared the common lot of mortals, but was still alive; that his access to the Almighty, and his being dearly beloved by him, rendered it easy for him to protect or recommend any of his faithful adherents. Though Turks never address any distinct prayers to their prophet, yet they pronounce his name, as if to invoke him, in the same manner as we say "O Lord!" and this was enough to draw upon them the severe reprehension of the Wahabys. They moreover visited his tomb, with the same devotion as they do the great temple of Mekka, and, when standing before it, uttered aloud their impious invocations, as the Wahabys called them; so that they fully deserved the opprobrious appellation of infidels, who associate an inferior divinity with the Almighty.

In similar respect are held many sheikhs, or saints, but not to the same extent. In every Turkish town are many tombs; and in almost every village at least one tomb of some renowned saint, whose exemplary life, (that is, great cunning or hypocrisy,) and sometimes great learning, had procured for him the reputation of sanctity Their countrymen thought it incumbent on them to honour their memory, by erecting small buildings, with cupolas or vaulted roofs over their tombs, and in these places particularly to offer up their prayers to the Divinity, in the belief that the saint would thus be more inclined to second their supplications before the throne of the Almighty. In fact, the

Mohammedan saints are venerated as highly as those of the Catholic church, and are said to perform as many miracles as the latter. The people of the East are extremely attached to their sheikhs; and in every town and village there is annually, on a fixed day, a festival in honour of its particular patron.* The Wahabys declared, that all men were equal in the eyes of God; that even the most virtuous could not intercede with him; and that it was, consequently, sinful to invoke departed saints, and to honour their mortal remains more than those of any other persons. Wherever the Wahabys carried their arms, they destroyed all the domes and ornamented tombs; a circumstance which served to inflame the fanaticism of their disciples, and to form a marked distinction between them and their opponents, which it has always been the policy of every founder of a sect to establish, and which was the more necessary

* Saints were formerly as much venerated in the Desert as in the towns. The Bedouins were accustomed to kill victims in honour of a saint, and to visit his tomb in a manner not much different from the pagan sacrifices to idols.

with the common mass of the Wahabys, who are not capable of judging accurately on the other points of dispute.

The destruction of cupolas and tombs of saints became the favourite taste of the Wahabys. In Hedjaz, Yemen, Mesopotamia, and Syria, this was always the first result of their victory; and as many domes formed the roofs of mosques, they were charged with destroying these also. At Mekka, not a single cupola was suffered to remain over the tomb of any renowned Arab: those even covering the birth-place of Mohammed, and of his grandsons, Hassan and Hosseyn, and of his uncle, Abou Táleb, and his wife, Khadydje, were all broken down. While in the act of destroying them, the Wahabys were heard to exclaim, " God have mercy upon those who destroyed, and none upon those who built them!" The Turks, who heard of these ravages, naturally believed that they were committed through disrespect for the persons to whose honour they had been erected, and disbelief in their sanctity. Even the large dome over the tomb of Mohammed, at Medinah, was destined to share a similar fate. Saoud had given orders that it should be demolished; but its solid structure defied the rude efforts of his soldiers; and after several of them had been killed by falling from the dome, the attempt was given up. This the inhabitants of Medinah declared to have been done through the interposition of Heaven.

The negligence of the far greater part of the Turks towards their religious laws, except what relates to prayer, purification, or fasting, was another subject against which the founder of the Wahaby sect inveighed. Alms to the poor, as enjoined by the law; the sumptuary regulations instituted by Mohammed; the severity and impartiality of justice, for which the first Khalifahs were so much distinguished; the martial spirit which was enjoined by the law to be constantly upheld against the enemies of the faith, or the infidels; the abstaining from whatever might inebriate, unlawful commerce with women, practices contrary to nature, and various others, were so many precepts not only entirely disregarded by the modern Turks, but openly violated with impunity. The scandalous conduct of many hadjys who polluted the sacred cities with their infamous lusts; the open license which the chiefs of the caravans gave to debauchery, and all the vices which follow in the train of pride and selfishness; the numerous acts of treachery and fraud perpetrated by the Turks, were all held up by the Wahabys as specimens of the general character of unreformed Muselmáns; and presented a sad contrast to the purity of morals and manners to which they themselves aspired, and to the humility with which the pilgrim is bound to approach the holy Kaaba. Enthusiastically attached to the primitive doctrines of his religion, justly indignant at seeing those doctrines corrupted by the present Muselmáns, and feeling, perhaps, no small degree of spite at having been treated with scorn in the Turkish towns, wherever he preached against disorders, Abd el Waháb, the founder of the sect, professed nothing but a desire to bring back his adherents to that state of religion, morals, and manners, which, as he had learnt from the best historical and theological works of his nation, prevailed when Islám was first promulgated in Arabia. As this code of law was evidently framed for Bedouins, the reformers found it the more easily re-adapted to the same people; and thus showed how little the foreigners, or Turks, had sacrificed their own northern manners to the true spirit of Islam. Not a single new precept was to be found in the Wahaby code. Abd el Waháb took as his sole guide the Koran and the Sunne (or the laws formed upon the traditions of Mohammed); and the only difference between his sect and orthodox Turks, however improperly so termed, is, that the Wahabys rigidly follow the same laws which the others neglect, or have ceased altogether to observe. To describe, therefore, the Wahaby religion, would be to recapitulate the Muselmán faith; and to show in what points this sect differs from the Turks, would be to give a list of all the abuses of which the latter are guilty. I am strongly warranted in giving this statement, by the opinion of several of the first olemas of Cairo. In the autumn of 1815, two envoys were sent to that city by the Wahaby chief, one of whom was a perfect Wahaby scholar. Mohammed Ali Pasha wished them to give an explanation of their tenets to the principal learned men of Cairo: they, in consequence, met repeatedly; and the Wahaby had invariably the best of the controversy, because he proved every proposition by a sentence of the Koran, and the Hadyth, or Tradition, the whole of which he knew by heart, and which were of course irrefragable authority. The olemas declared, that they could find no heresy in the Wahabys; and as this was a declaration made in spite of themselves, it is the less to be suspected. A book had also been received at Cairo, containing various treatises on religious subjects, written by Abd el Wahab himself: it was read by many olemas, and they declared unanimously, that if such were the opinions of the Wahabys, they themselves belonged altogether to that creed.

As the fanatic mob of a new sect can seldom be impressed with the true spirit of its founder, it happened that the greater part of the followers of Abd el Wahab considered as chief points of doctrine such as were rather accessories, and thus caused their enemies to form very erroneous notions of the supposed new religion. Next to the war which they declared against saints, their fanaticism was principally turned against dress, and the smoking of tobacco. The rich Turkish costume is little in accordance with the precepts of the Sunne, where silk is absolutely prohibited, as well as gold and silver, except the latter, in small quantity. The Wahabys beheld the gaudy robes of the Turkish pilgrims with disdain; and as they knew that the Prophet had worn an abba like them, and had prohibited sumptuous apparel, they considered it to be as necessary to follow his mode of dress, as his moral precepts. It was by the dress that Wahabys could be immediately recognised in Arabia. An Arab who had not embraced this creed, would assuredly have some part of his dress of silk; either the kerchief round his head would be interwoven with silk, or his gown would be sewed with silk. Respecting the smoking of tobacco, it is well known that many Turkish olemas have repeatedly, in their writings, declared it to be a forbidden practice. One of the four orthodox sects of the Muselmáns, the Malekys, have declared it "hateful." A great number of olemas in every part of Turkey abstain from it on religious principles. The Wahaby wished also to prevent the smoking of intoxicating plants, much used in the East, being directly against the Koran, but which could not well be prevented, while the pipe was suffered. He must, at the same time, have been aware, that his followers, in making so great a sacrifice as abstinence from smoking, would naturally become the more bitter enemies to all those who still indulged in that luxury, and had not yet embraced their creed. The prohibition of tobacco has been one of the principal means of inflaming the minds of the Wahabys against the Turks: it has become a rallying word to the proselytes; but of all the precepts taught by the reformers, it has been the most reluctantly complied with by the Arabs. Another prohibited act is praying over the rosary, a general practice with moslems, though not founded on the law. The Wahabys declared it to be an unwarrantable practice, and abolished it. It has been stated that they likewise prohibited the drinking of coffee; this, however, is not the fact, they have always used it to an immoderate degree.

It is much to be doubted whether Abd el Wahab, when he preached reform at Derayeh, had any idea of establishing a new dynasty to reign over the proselytes of Arabia. The strength of his own and of his relations' families did not authorise him in undertaking such a measure, which seems to have gained ground only during the life of Abd el Azyz, the son of Mohammed Ibn Saoud. In delivering his new doctrines to the Arabs, it cannot be denied that Abd el Waháb conferred on them a great blessing; nor was the form of government that ensued unfavourable to the interests and prosperity of the whole Arabian nation. Whether the commonly received doctrine considered as orthodox, or that of the Wahabys, should be pronounced the true Mohammedan religion, is, after all, a matter of little consequence; but it became important to suppress that infidel indifference which had pervaded all Arabia and a great part of

Turkey, and which has a more baneful effect on the morals of a nation than the decided acknowledgment even of a false religion. The merit, therefore, of the Wahabys, in my opinion, is not that they purified the existing religion, but that they made the Arabs strictly observe the positive precepts of one certain religion; for although the Bedouins at all times devoutly worshipped the Divinity, yet the deistical principles alone could not be deemed sufficient to instruct a nation so wild and ungovernable in the practice of morality and justice.

A desire of reducing the Arabs to the state in which they were when the founder of their religion existed, naturally induced Abd el Waháb and his successors to alter likewise their political condition as soon as they perceived that their proselytes increased. Mohammed, and after him the Khalifahs, were the spiritual as well as the political leaders of their nation; and the code of Muselmán law shows in every page how necessary is the existence of a supreme chief in religious and in civil affairs. Nedjd, which became the principal seat of the

Wahaby power, was divided into a number of small territories, cities, and villages, totally independent of each other, and constantly engaged in warfare. No law but that of the strongest was acknowledged either in the open country or within the walls of towns, and personal security was always purchased at the price of individual property. Besides this, the wild freedom of the neighbouring Bedouin tribes, their endless wars and predatory expeditions, rendered Nedjd and the surrounding country a scene of perpetual disorder and bloodshed. It was not until after many hard struggles that Abd el Azyz extended at last his religion over the whole of Nedjd; and being then no longer the chief of a tribe, but of a province, he assumed the supreme power, and assimilated his authority to that which was exercised by the first followers of Mohammed.

To enslave his countrymen would have been a fruitless attempt; he left them in the enjoyment of their freedom, but obliged them to live in peace, to respect property, and to obey the decisions of the law.

Thus in process of time the Wahaby chief

became governor of the greater part of Arabia; his government was free, because it was founded upon the system of a Bedouin commonwealth. He was the head of all the sheikhs of tribes whose respective politics he directed, while all the Arabs remained within their tribes completely independent and at liberty, except that they were now obliged to observe the strict sense of the law, and liable to punishment if they infringed it. Formerly an Arab acknowledged no rule but his own will; he was forced by the Wahaby chief to obey the ancient Muselmán laws. These enjoined him to give tithes or tribute to the great chief, and that he should be at all times ready to join his ranks in any expedition against heretics or infidels. It was not allowed, that in a dispute with his neighbours an appeal should be made to arms, and a tribunal was fixed, before which all litigations should be decided. Such were the main objects of the Wahaby chiefs: tribute, military conscription, internal peace, and rigid administration of justice. They had completely succeeded in carrying these measures into execution, and seemed to be firmly established, when the efforts of Mohammed Aly, and his gold, rather than the valour of his troops, weakened their power and reduced them to the state in which they had been several years before. I shall now enter into further details concerning this interesting government; details founded on the most accurate statements that I could obtain from many well-informed people in Hedjaz.

Of Saoud's person and family.

Saoud, chief propagator of the new doctrine, was eldest son of Abd el Azyz, who was assassinated in the year 1803. Besides Saoud, his mother, the daughter of Abd el Wahab, had two sons, Abderrahman and Abdallah. Saoud died, aged forty-five or fifty, in April 1814, of a fever, at Derayeh; and to his death may be attributed the misfortunes which befell his nation soon after. He is said to have been a remarkably handsome man, with one of those fine countenances for which his family has been distinguished. He wore a longer beard than is generally seen among Bedouins, and so much hair about his mouth that the people of Derayeh called him *Abou Showâreb*, or the " Father of Mustachios."

All the Arabs, even his enemies, praise Saoud for his wisdom in counsel and his skill in deciding litigations; he was very learned in the Muselmán law; and the rigour of his justice, although it disgusted many of his chiefs, endeared him to the great mass of his Arabs. From the time that his reign began, he never fought personally in battle; but always directed his army from a position at some distance in the rear. It is related by the Arabs, that he once fought in a battle when only twelve years old, by the side of his father Abd el Azyz.

By his first wife, now dead, he had eight children; of these the oldest is Abdallah, who during his father's life-time occupied the second place in his dominions, and after his death succeeded to the supreme government. It is related that at the early age of five years Abdallah could gallop his mare; and he is more eminent for courage than his father, as he made it a constant rule to fight every where in person. During the life of Saoud, the mental qualities of his son, Abdallah, were described as of the first order, and he was regarded as a prodigy of wisdom and sagacity; but the measures which he adopted in opposing Mohammed Aly seem to prove that he by no means possessed such abilities as his father in those respects. He is esteemed in the Desert on account of his liberality and his social manners. He married a girl of the Záb Arabs, in the province of Hassa. Of his brethren, the most celebrated among the Arabs, is *Faysal*, reputed the handsomest man in Derayeh, and the most amiable. To him the Arabs are much attached. He has fought many battles in Hedjaz against the Turkish troops. *Nászer* was the favourite son of Saoud; he fell in an expedition against Maskat. *El Turky* often commanded flying corps of Wahabys in Irak and towards Syria. By his third wife, Saoud had three sons, *Omar*, *Ibrahím*, and *Fcheyd*.

Saoud never permitted his children to exercise any influence in public affairs, except Abdallah, who participated in all his counsels. But he was extremely attached to them. The inhabitants of Mekka still relate with pleasure, that at the time of the pilgrimage, Saoud was once sitting under the gate of the Kaaba, while his people were covering that edifice with the new cloth, and numerous pilgrims were engaged in their sacred walk around it. At that moment the wife of his son Feheyd appeared, holding in her arms one of his young children. She had just arrived at Mekka for the pilgrimage, and hastened towards Saoud that she might present to him the infant, whom he had not before seen. He took it from her, kissed it affectionately, and in presence of all the assembled pilgrims pressed it to his bosom for a considerable time.

Besides his wife, Saoud had, according to the custom of great people in Nedjd, several Abyssinian female slaves or concubines; he resided with all his family in a large mansion built by his father on the declivity of the mountain, a little above the town of Derayeh. All his children, with their families, and all his brothers had their separate ranges of apartments in that building. Of his brothers he is said to have entertained some jealousy; he never appointed them to any post of confidence, nor did he permit them to leave Derayeh. In this house he kept his treasures, and received all those who came on business to Derayeh. There the great emírs, or chiefs of considerable tribes, were lodged and feasted on their arrival, while people of inferior rank resided with their acquaintances in the town; but if they came on business they might dine or sup at the chief's house, and bring from it a daily allowance of food for their horses or camels. It may easily be conceived, that the palace was constantly full of guests.

Saoud granted ready admission to every person; but to obtain a private interview without his especial desire, was rather difficult. He had several Egyptians who served as porters, and for a bribe would admit people into the interior apartments at unusual hours. The surest mode of obtaining private access was to wait before the inner apartment until some great sheikh passed, and to enter with his attendants. Saoud gave public audiences early in the morning, between three and six o'clock in the afternoon, and again late in the evening. After supper he regularly assembled in the great room all his sons who happened to be at Derayeh; and all those, who were desirous of paying court to him, joined this family circle. One of the olemas then read a few pages of the Koran, or the Traditions of Mohammed, and explained the text according to the commentaries of the best writers. After him, other olemas delivered lectures in the same manner, and Saoud himself always closed the meeting by taking the book and explaining every difficult passage. It is said that he equalled, or perhaps excelled, any of the olemas in his knowledge of religious controversy and of the law in general. His eloquence was universally admired; his voice remarkably sonorous and sweet at the same time, which made the Arabs say, that "his words all reached the heart." Upon those occasions, Saoud was the only speaker; but it often happened that points of law were to be discussed, and these sometimes excited his impatience and induced him to argue with great vehemence, deriding his adversary, and taunting him for his ignorance in controversy. Thus, having continued about an hour, Saoud generally concluded by saying, " *Wa Allahou aálem*"— " God knows best ;" and those who had no particular business understood that expression as the signal for departure, and persons who had business with him remained until two hours after sun-set: these assemblies took place every evening.

Saoud was extremely indignant when any Arab endeavoured to deceive him by a falsehood. On such occasions, he sometimes seized a stick, and belaboured the man himself; but of these passionate fits he soon repented, and desired the by-standers always to interpose and prevent him from striking any person whenever they should see him angry; this was frequently done, and he expressed his thanks for the interference.

During his residence at Derayeh, Saoud very rarely left his house, except when he went on Fridays to the neighbouring mosque. The Arabs imputed this seclusion to fear, supposing that he apprehended the fate by which his father perished—assassination; and he certainly had enemies enough among the Arabs, anxious to avenge the blood of relations shed by him, and ready to conspire against his life, if they could see any possibility of succeeding in their attempts to kill him. But his friends declared, that he was occupied the whole day at home in study. It is well known, that for several years after the death of his father, Saoud constantly wore a coat of mail under his shirt. The inhabitants of Mekka relate, that during his stay in that city he was always surrounded by a chosen guard, and that no stranger dared to approach him alone. He would not even go to the great mosque, nor perform the circuit of the holy Kaaba without a numerous train of followers: and he chose his seat during prayers in the mosque, not as persons of distinction generally do, in the *Mekám el Hanbaly*, but mounted the roof of the *Bír*, or Well of *Zemzem*, as a more safe position, and he prayed upon that roof which forms the *Mekám el Shafey*.

Not only in his own palace, but throughout

his dominions, he desired that persons should remain seated when he appeared; and at his evening assemblies (*madjlis*), every body sat down where he could find a convenient place, although it was generally understood that the great emírs should take their seats next to Saoud. His younger sons sat among the crowd, paying due attention to all that was said, but never speaking themselves. The Arabs who entered, usually shook hands with Saoud, having previously hailed him with the salutation of peace, and he politely inquired after the health and affairs of all whom he knew in the room. The great sheikh, on arriving at Saoud's residence, exchanged a kiss with him, according to Bedouin custom. In addressing him, no pompous title was used; the people merely said, "O Saoud!" or "O father of Abdallah!" or "O father of Mustachios!" he, too, called every man by his name without any ceremonious or complimentary phrases, which are so numerous among Eastern nations in general.

In his dress, Saoud did not affect any distinction from his own Arabs; he only wore an abba, a shirt, and a keffie, or head-kerchief:

yet it is said that he chose these articles from among the finest that Derayeh could afford; that he was scrupulously clean, and had his keffie constantly perfumed with civet.

The principal expense of Saoud's establishment was for his guests and his horses; he is said to have kept no less than two thousand horses and mares as his own property. Of these, three or four hundred were always at Derayeh, and the others in the province of El Hassa, where the clover pasturage is excellent. The finest mares of Arabia were in his possession. Some of those he had taken from their original owners, either as a punishment for misconduct, or as a fine, but he had purchased many at very considerable prices; it is known that he paid for one mare a sum equivalent to five hundred and fifty or six hundred pounds sterling.

To each of his sons he allowed a retinue of one hundred or a hundred and fifty horsemen. Abdallah, during the life of his father, had above three hundred. To these may be added numerous *delouls*, or swift camels, of which Saoud kept the best breed in Arabia.

The members of his own household and the

strangers whom he fed every day, amounted to between four and five hundred persons. Rice, boiled corn (*borghol*), dates, and mutton, constituted the principal dishes. Saoud permitted his grown-up sons and the great sheikhs to eat with himself: their usual food was rice and mutton; common strangers were treated with borghol and dates. From all that I could learn of his manner of living and the prices of provisions in Nedjd, it would appear that his whole establishment (exclusive of the body-guard which is paid out of the public treasury) cost him annually from ten to twelve thousand pounds sterling. Contrary to Turkish and Bedouin customs, Saoud never celebrated any circumcision feasts in his house, because, as he said, no such feasts ever took place at the first propagation of Islám. Yet he allowed his Arabs to amuse themselves on those occasions. He also observed with great splendour the nuptials of his children. When his son, Feheyd, married his cousin, the wedding-feast at Derayeh lasted for three days. On the first day, the girl's father, Saoud's brother, treated the guests, consisting of all the male inhabitants of the town and a number of strangers, with the meat of forty she-camels and five hundred sheep. On the second day, Saoud himself slaughtered for his guests one hundred she-camels and eight hundred sheep. On the third day, another of his brothers entertained all the company.

Saoud kept a number of black slaves in his house. He never would permit any of his wives or concubines to suckle their own male children; but for that purpose had always in readiness some wet-nurses, generally chosen among his Abyssinian slaves. A similar practice is prevalent among the sherifs of Mekka, who educate their little children among the neighbouring Bedouin tribes, never keeping them above eight days in their own father's house. After the same fashion, Mohammed was educated among the tribe of *Adouán*.

Wahaby Government.

This is an aristocracy, at the head of which stands the family of Saoud. He divided his dominions into several governorships, which included the Arab tribes who have become settlers. Every great Bedouin tribe has also a governor or sheikh; and subordinate to them are various minor chiefs. The great Bedouin sheikhs, to whom the minor tribes are obliged to pay deference, receive from the Wahaby chief the honorary title of *Emír el Omera.* The principal governorships are those of the districts *el Hassa el Aredh,* (which Saoud took into his own hands, Derayeh being the capital of that province,) *el Kasym, Djebel Shammar, el Harameyn,* (Mekka and Medinah,) *el Hedjáz,* (signifying in the Bedouin acceptation, the mountains southward of Tayf,) and *el Yemen.* The governors or emírs of those provinces execute public justice, but are not the judges; for Saoud has every where placed his own kadhys. The authority of those emírs over the Arabs is very limited, not much exceeding that which an independent Bedouin sheikh possesses, except that he can enforce obedience to the law by imprisoning the transgressor and fining him for non-compliance. If he himself commit injustice, an appeal is made to the great chief;

hence Derayeh is constantly filled with Arabs coming from the remotest quarters to plead against their sheikhs The principal duty incumbent on the latter (besides the execution of justice) is to recruit troops for the Wahaby army, and to assist the tax-gatherers.

In the time of war, the chiefs of these provinces, as well as the great Bedouin sheikhs, form a council; in time of peace, Saoud consulted none but the olemas of Derayeh. These belong principally to the family of Abd el Wahab, founder of the sect; they are numerous at Derayeh, and possess considerable influence. That family is called "*Oulad es' Sheikh.*" I do not exactly know what positive rights or privileges they possess; but it is certain, that Saoud communicated to them every important affair before a final decision was given. The Wahaby chief may seem an absolute master, but he knows too well the spirit of his Arabs to attempt governing with despotic sway. The liberties of individuals are maintained as in former times; but he appears to administer justice rather as a potent sheikh than as the lord of Arabia. He is, in fact, under the control of his own governors, all persons of great influence in their respective provinces, who would soon declare themselves independent were he to treat them with injustice Instances of this kind have maintained that pirit of resistance against arbitrary power, to which the Bedouins never yield. The governors of provinces are controlled in their authority by a number of lesser sheikhs; and we accordingly find many small clans always ready to defend their cause against the tyranny of the great chief, who, in uniting them all under one system of government, has succeeded, after violent struggles, in establishing an order of things in Arabia, equally advantageous to public security and to private interests.

The Waháby government is now (1816) hereditary in the family of the Saouds. While Abd el Azyz lived, the principal sheikhs were required to swear allegiance to his son Saoud, who succeeded to the supreme authority, on his father's death, without opposition. In the same manner the sheikhs afterwards swore fidelity to Abdallah, while his father Saoud was still living. The Arabs, however, do not think it necessary that the chieftainship should descend from father to son. Saoud might have nominated one of his brothers to succeed him, and so far we may presume that the same system prevails at Derayeh as all over the Desert in electing the sheikh of a tribe.

The chief Waháby appoints and removes at his pleasure the sheikhs of cities, districts, and tribes; but he generally confirms the election made by the Arabs themselves; and if a sheikh proves attached to his cause, he always permits his son or brother to succeed him.

Administration of Justice.

All the open country of Arabia, and all the towns of the interior were formerly subject to the same disorderly state of law which still prevails among those tribes that have not submitted to the Wahabys, and which I have described in my account of the Bedouins. Abd el Azyz and Saoud taught their Arabs to obey the law, to maintain public peace, and in their disputes to abide by the decision of a tribunal, without any appeal to arms. Abd el Azyz was the first who sent kadhys into all the districts under his sway. He chose them among the most able and upright of his learned men, and assigned to them annual allowances from the public treasury, forbidding them to accept fees or bribes from contending parties. Those kadhys were to judge according to the laws of the *Korán* and the *Sunne*. All the Arabs were to state their subjects of litigation before them, but might afterwards appeal to the supreme chief.

The next step was to secure the country against robbers. Before Abd el Azyz had acquired sufficient power, the whole of Nedjd, and, indeed, of Arabia, was overrun in every direction by hostile parties, and the great number of independent states rendered it impossible to establish a firm internal peace. Abd el Azyz, and, still more, his son Saoud, made the Arabs responsible for every robbery committed within their territory, should the robber be unknown; and those who were sufficiently strong to repel or resist a hostile invasion of a camp or town, and wanted the inclination or courage to do so, were punished by a fine equivalent to the amount of cattle or other property taken away by the robbers. Thus every tribe was rendered vigilant in protecting its neighbours, as well as strangers passing through their territory. So that both public and private robberies almost totally ceased among the settlers as well as Bedouins of Arabia, who formerly delighted in nothing so much as in pilfering and plundering. For the first time, perhaps, since the days of Mohammed, a single merchant might traverse the Desert of Arabia with perfect safety, and the Bedouins slept without any apprehension that their cattle would be carried off by nocturnal depredators.

The two Wahaby chiefs seem to have been particularly anxious that their Arabs should renounce the long-established custom of taking into their own hands the punishment of an enemy, and inflicting retaliation. They, therefore, constantly endeavoured, more especially Saoud, to abolish the system of blood-revenge, and to render the Arabs content with a stipulated price, payable for the blood of a relation. But in this respect, the chief was never able to obtain complete success; he has frequently compelled the sufferer's family to accept the fine, if offered by the homicide's party; but if any act of revenge has taken place before he can give orders respecting the fine, he does not punish the man who availed himself of the old Arab rights.

If disputes arise among his people and occasion blows, and if the relations of both parties espouse respectively the cause of their friends (as is usual in Arabia), shedding blood in the affray, Saoud without any mercy condemns all those who meddled on the occasion, and punishes them either by taking away their horses, camels, and arms, or else by the confiscation of their property to the public treasury.

In a quarrel among Arabs, should one draw his dagger and wound another, Saoud levied a heavy fine upon the by-standers for allowing the matter to proceed so far. If, notwithstanding the laws against war, two tribes commence hostilities, Saoud immediately sends messengers to the sheikhs, and insists upon a reconciliation, levying a fine from each tribe, and obliging them to pay to each other the price of blood for the lives of those who perished in the first onset. Tribes were commanded to bring their public disputes always before the tribunal of Saoud, whose authority was so dreaded, that a single Negro slave of his household has been known to arrest, by his order, some great sheikh in the midst of his own camp, and bring him as a prisoner to Derayeh.

Saoud was acknowledged to be a man of incorruptible justice; but in his sentences against transgressors rather too severe. His great penetration enabled him soon to discover when a witness prevaricated; and this he punished always in an exemplary manner. His punishments, however, were not cruel; and I have been assured that, since the death of his father, only four or five men have been put to death at Derayeh. As the Bedouins rarely possess any money, he fines them in horses, camels, and sheep. It is this severity which has excited against him so many enemies among his own Arabs. He never respects the protection given to a delinquent by other Arabs. He abolished the laws of dakheil (or protection) all over his dominions, as far as they might be used in screening a person from the hand of justice. If an Arab has killed another, he may seek dakheil at a friend's, to save himself from the immediate vengeance of the deceased man's relations; but he can remain under that protection only until the law claims him, and he must then be given up.

The great sheikhs grant a kind of protection to delinquents accused of petty crimes. An Arab, in such a case, and afraid of appearing before Saoud, places himself under the protection of some sheikh who possesses influence with the chief. This sheikh intercedes, and generally prevails on Saoud to remit the punishment, or commute it for a small fine.

The offence which Saoud had most frequently to punish was the intercourse of his Arabs with heretics. At the time that the Wahaby creed was first instituted, the most positive orders had been given to interdict all communication between the Wahabys and other nations who had not yet adopted the new doctrine; for it was said, that the sword alone was to be used in argument with the latter. As the inhabitants of Nedjd, however, were much in the habit of visiting Medinah, Damascus, Baghdad, and the adjacent countries, they continually disobeyed those orders; so that at last Saoud found it necessary to relax his severity on that subject. He even tacitly connived, in the last period of the Syrian hadj, at his Arabs transporting provisions for the caravans, and took himself one dollar for every camel, belonging to his people, so employed; but except in this carrying business of the hadj, he never would allow any of his Arabs to trade with Syria or Baghdad until after 1810, when the Egyptian expedition began. Yet the law existed, that if a Wahaby, whether Bedouin or merchant, should be found on the road going towards any heretic country, (which the direction of the road, and nature of the loads would prove,) his whole property in goods and cattle should be confiscated to the public treasury. But in returning from the heretic country, his property is respected.

Those arbitrary impositions, called *avanius* in the Levant, are wholly unknown in the

Wahaby dominions, where no individuals were ever required to pay more than what he owed to the tax-gatherers, or a fine to the treasury for some offence. Wealthy individuals are perfectly secure from the rapacity of government; and this perhaps is the only part of the East where such is the case. The rich merchants of Mekka, whose warehouses contained the finest Bedouin clothes, were never obliged to pay the smallest sum, nor even to give any valuable presents to Saoud.

The Arabs, however, murmur at a kind of forced requisition, in the frequent orders of their chief to join him on his expeditions against the heretics. In this case the Arabs must find their own food and camels, or horses, and receive in return no emolument but whatever booty they may be able to take. Such expeditions, are therefore very expensive to them. On the other hand, any man who has incurred the displeasure of Saoud, by some minor offence, is sure to conciliate him by joining in his expeditions.

The great security which resulted from this rigid administration of justice, naturally pleased those who were most exposed to depredations and disorders of any kind. The settlers, therefore, of Nedjd, Hedjaz, and Yemen, became most sincerely attached to the new system, because they had suffered most from the defects of the old. Caravans of any extent, loaded with the produce of the ground, passed unmolested through those parts of the country; nor were the people ever afraid that their crops should be cut up, or destroyed by the wandering tribes. The latter, on the contrary, who had always lived by robberies and attacks on others, found it much more difficult to obey a government whose first principles directly opposed their mode of subsistence. It is therefore not surprising that some of the great Bedouin tribes hesitated to adopt the Wahaby creed, until it was forced upon them by a superior power; and they have proved, by frequent revolts, how impatient they are of the check which they have experienced in their manner of living; to which must be added, their repugnance with respect to paying the tribute.

If Saoud was known to be a very severe judge in cases of transgression, and implacable towards his enemies, he was equally celebrated for the warmth and sincerity of his friendship, and his regard for old and faithful adherents. Any sheikh who has evinced his attachment to Saoud, might rely on his constant protection and help under all misfortunes, even to the full indemnification for every loss, however considerable, that he might incur in his service.

The greatest punishment inflicted by order of the Wahaby chief is the shaving of the culprit's beard. This is done only with persons of distinction, or rebel sheikhs, and is to some a disgrace more intolerable than death. An Arab thus shaved endeavours to conceal himself from view until his beard grows again. An anecdote related on this subject shows the real character of an Arab. Saoud had long wished to purchase the mare of a sheikh belonging to the tribe of Beni Shammar, but the owner refused to sell her for any sum of money. At this time, a sheikh of the Kahtán Arabs had been sentenced to lose his beard for some offence When the barber produced his razor in presence of Saoud, the sheikh exclaimed, "O Saoud, take the mare of the Shammary as a ransom for my beard!'" The punishment was remitted; the sheikh was allowed to go and bargain for the mare, which cost him two thousand five hundred dollars, swearing that no sum of money could have induced him to part with her, had it not been to save the beard of a noble Kahtány. But this is a rare example; for Saoud frequently refused considerable offers of money, to remit the punishment of shaving.

I shall here notice some Wahaby laws, founded upon the Korán, and sayings of Mohammed.

A haramy, or robber, is obliged to return the stolen goods, or their value; but if the offence is not attended with circumstances of violence, he escapes without further punishment, except a fine to the treasury. If a door be broken open in committing the robbery, the thief's hand is cut off.

One who kills his antagonist in a dispute with dagger or pistol is condemned to death: if he kills him by a blow of a stick or stone, it is deemed man-slaughter; and he only pays the price of blood, as having not been armed with any deadly weapon.

The price of blood among the Wahabys is fixed at one hundred she-camels, according to the rate established by Abou Beker. Saoud valued every camel at eight Spanish dollars; and the fixed sum is now eight hundred dollars.

Whoever curses a Wahaby, or calls him "infidel," incurs very heavy penalties. The terms of insult are measured among the Wahabys with great exactness; the worst (not amenable to the law) is to call a man "dog." The common insult is to say, "O doer" (that is doer of evil or mischief), or "O leaver-off" (that is, O leaver-off of religious and social duties).

The stocks, called *debabe*, in which the feet of prisoners are confined, is only for the lower class. Saoud has a prison in his own mansion for persons of quality; those especially who, having been sentenced to pay a certain sum, plead poverty, and refuse to comply. In some cases, they are imprisoned until they pay.

The neglect of religious duty is always severely punished. I have already mentioned the penalty for omission of prayers. When

Saoud took Medinah, he ordered some of his people, after prayers in the mosque, to call over the names of all the grown-up inhabitants of the town who were to answer individually: he then commanded them to attend prayers regularly; and if any one absented himself two or three times, Saoud sent some of his Arabs to beat the man in his own house. At Mekka, when the hour of prayer arrived, he ordered his people to patrol the streets, armed with large sticks, and to drive all the inhabitants by force into the mosque; a harsh proceeding, but justified by the notorious irreligion of the Mekkans. Saoud has always been extremely punctual in performing the pilgrimage to Mekka. Whenever it was in his power he repaired to that holy place, accompanied by thousands of his Arabs, men and women. His last pilgrimage was performed in the year 1812.

Saoud endeavoured to check among his people the frequent practice of divorce, so pernicious to social and moral habits. Whenever he heard an Arab say, "I swear by the divorce" (that is, from my wife), he ordered that the man should be beaten. To break the fast of Ramadhan, without some legitimate excuse, subjected a man to capital punishment. Abd el Azyz (who was, however, more rigid than his son) once put an Arab to death for that offence. The smoking of tobacco publicly is forbidden; but it is well known that all the people of Nedjd continue this practice in their houses; and even the Wahabys, in their camps, at night. On the capture of Mekka, Saoud ordered all the inhabitants to take their Persian pipes (called *shíshe* by the Arabs) to a green piece of ground, before the house where he resided; and having formed them into a vast heap, he set them on fire, together with all the tobacco that could be found in the shops. Some time after, one of his retinue informed him in public, that the Mekkans disregarded his orders, and still smoked. "Where did you see them smoke?" asked Saoud. "In their own houses," answered the informer. "Do you not know," replied the chief, "that it is written, 'do not spy out the secrets of the houses of the faithful?'" Having quoted this sentence of the Koran, he ordered the informer to be bastinadoed, and no further notice was taken of the private smoking.

The Mekkans still remember, with gratitude, the excellent police observed by Saoud's troops during his frequent visits to Mekka; especially on his first taking the town. With the same vigilance he watches over his soldiers on an expedition; and whoever receives from him the word *Amán*, or safe-conduct, may be perfectly secure from any misconduct of the troops. It was mentioned, as an instance of the Wahabys' good faith, that some of them were often seen in the temple at Mekka, looking out for the owners of lost articles which they had found, and were desirous of returning.

Saoud always protected trade in his dominions, provided that it was not carried on with those whom he called heretical Muselmáns. The principal trade of Nedjd is in provisions; and there the tribes from the interior of the Desert purchased what they required; and as years of dearth often occur, the rich people hoard up great quantities of corn. With these Saoud never interfered;

and in times of scarcity he allowed them to sell at their own prices, however they might distress the poor; for he said, that Mohammed never forbade merchants to derive from their capitals as much profit as they possibly could obtain.

Usury, and even lending money on interest (which is not uncommon among the Bedouins), he prohibited under severe penalties, as contrary to the express tenor of the law. If money was lent, the conditions were generally to share the chances of loss, and to take one half of the profits.

The Wahabys have no particular coin. Dollars are in general currency; and articles of little value are estimated by measures of corn, or purchased with old copper money of the imáms of Yemen. Venetian zequins are likewise taken, but no Turkish coin whatever. During the late war in Hedjaz, when the Wahabys killed and stripped any Turkish soldiers, and found some piastres in their pockets, they always threw them with indignation on the ground.

Revenues.

The Wahaby revenues have been established upon a plan similar to that which prevailed in the time of Mohammed. They consist in—

1. One fifth of the booty taken from the heretics. This portion must be set aside for the chief, whether he or one of his officers was present on the expedition; and the sheikh of the most distant tribe is answerable for the remittance of it, however small or considerable the amount may be. Saoud never attempted to withhold from his soldiers the remaining four fifths. In common warfare with Arabs (when cities are not plundered), the booty consists generally of horses, camels, and sheep; those are sold to the highest bidder immediately after the battle. The money thus obtained is distributed among the troops. A cavalry soldier has three shares (one for himself, and two, as the Arabs say, for his mare); every camel-rider has one share, (before Saoud's time he had two,) every foot-soldier one share. If in battle a Wahaby

should kill a trooper of the enemy, and get possession of his mare, he is allowed to keep it as his own property, and the recompence of his valour. I need not here repeat, that Mohammed took the fifth part of all booty.

2. The tribute; or, as it is called by the Wahabys, "the Alms." A fundamental law of Islam is the giving of these alms. Mohammed regulated the amount which is observed by the Wahaby legislator. Similar alms are prescribed to the Turks also, but the distribution is left to every man's own conscience; whereas the Wahabys are obliged to deliver them, for distribution, to their chief. The Muselman law has minutely fixed what proportion the alms are to bear with respect to the property; and the Wahabys have not made any alteration in this arrangement. The sums paid in proportion to horses, sheep, and camels, are according to the precepts of the Sunne, and may be seen detailed in D'Ohhson's excellent work. Saoud divided the tribute from his subjects into two parts; that from the Bedouins flows wholly into his private treasury; but the alms from inhabitants of towns, or cultiva-

tors, are appropriated to the public treasury, or "*Beit el Mál.*"

From fields watered by rains only, Saoud takes a tithe of the produce; from fields fertilised by the water of wells or of fountains, which it is laborious and expensive to draw, he takes but one twentieth of the produce.

The merchants pay yearly two and a half per cent on their capital, and are obliged to state its amount upon oath to the collector. It is, however, well known that they seldom return an account of more than one fourth of their property. A merchant of Khadera, in the province of Kasym, had been robbed of three thousand dollars in cash. He applied for assistance to Saoud, who directed the clerk of the Beit el Mál, or treasury, at Khadera, to ascertain how much the merchant had reported his property to be worth; and it appeared that he had only stated it as being one thousand dollars. For this false return, Saoud confiscated the merchant's mare and camels.

These alms, or *zeka*, are peculiarly galling to the Arabs under Saoud's authority, as they were formerly free from taxes of any kind. Distant tribes have frequently revolted on account of them, and driven away the collectors. Nothing but compulsion or necessity could ever induce a Bedouin to admit of taxation. It is likewise the exemption from these zeka which rendered the Hedjáz Bedouins less hostile to the cause of Mohammed Aly Pasha than they otherwise might have been; for his first measure was to declare, that not only the Bedouins, but all the settled inhabitants of Hedjaz, should be wholly free from taxes.

3. The most considerable portion of the Wahaby chief's revenues are derived from his own domains. He has established it as a rule, that whenever any of his districts or cities rise in rebellion, he plunders them for the first offence; for the second rebellion, he not only plunders but confiscates them, and all their land, to the public treasury. He then bestows some parts of them on strangers, but leaves most in the hands of the former proprietors, who now become merely his farmers, and are obliged to pay, according to circumstances, either one third or one half

of the produce. The property of those who took the most active part in the rebellion is farmed out to others, while they themselves either fly or are put to death.

As the Arabs did not adopt the Wahaby system until after repeated struggles, considerable districts were thus confiscated to the chief, and if ever he resume his power in Hedjaz, he will seize in like manner on the property of all who had joined Mohammed Aly. At present most of the landed property in Nedjd belongs to the Beit el Mál, or treasury; that of Kasym, whose inhabitants have been constantly in rebellion, is entirely held in farm; and many villages of Hedjaz, and the mountains towards Yemen, are attached also to the treasury.

4. Fines levied for trespasses against the law. The crime of disobedience is generally expiated by pecuniary fines. It is a maxim in the Wahaby courts, that an Arab who falsely accuses another must pay a fine to the treasury.

All these revenues, except the alms, or zeka, from the Bedouins, are deposited in the public treasury, or Beit el Mál. Every city or village of any note has its own treasury, into which the inhabitants pay their quotas. Every treasury has a writer, or clerk, sent by the Wahaby chief with orders to prevent the sheikh of the place from partaking in illicit gain from the revenue. The sheikhs are not allowed to collect nor to account for the money paid. These funds are appropriated to public services, and are therefore divided into four parts. One fourth is sent to the great treasury at Derayeh; one fourth is dedicated to the relief of paupers in the district of the Beit el Mál; for the pay of olemas who are to instruct the kadhys and the children; for keeping the mosques in repair, digging public wells, &c. One half is expended for the benefit of indigent soldiers, who are furnished with provisions when they set out on an expedition, or, in case of necessity, with camels; also for the entertainment of guests. The money thus allowed for guests is paid into the hands of the sheikhs, who keep a sort of public houses, where all strangers may halt and be fed gratis; it is thought just that the whole community should contribute towards their expenses. Thus Ibn

Aly, the sheikh of Beni Shammar, in Djebel Shammar, has every year from the treasury of his province, two hundred camel-loads of corn, two hundred loads of dates, and one thousand Spanish dollars; with this money he purchases meat, butter, and coffee; and the whole is expended in the entertainment of from two to three hundred strangers of all descriptions, who are received and fed every day in his public rooms.

From the great treasury of Derayeh, sums are applied to the relief of Saoud's faithful subjects, whose property had been taken by the enemy. Derayeh is always full of Arabs who apply to Saoud for the restitution of some part at least of their lost property. If Saoud knows the man to be a sincere Wahaby, he generally pays him to the amount of one third. Other sums are given from that treasury to Arabs who have lost their cattle through disease or accidents. If upon an expedition the mare or camel (deloul) of a soldier has been killed, or dies, and that booty has been taken, Saoud most commonly gives another mare or camel to the soldier; if no booty has been taken, the Arab must bear the loss.

Besides what is paid to the sheikhs of districts, towns, or villages, for the entertainment of guests, the Bedouin sheikhs receive annual presents from the treasury of Derayeh as tokens of Saoud's good-will. These donations vary from fifty to three hundred dollars, and are bestowed in imitation of a similar practice of Mohammed.

The collectors of revenue (called *nawáb*, or *mezekki*, or *aámil*) are sent every year from Derayeh to the different districts or tribes, and receive a certain sum for their trouble and expenses on the journey. Thus every collector sent from Derayeh to the Bedouins of the Syrian Desert, receives seventy-five dollars. The sheikhs, as I have already mentioned, are not allowed any concern in the taxes. When the collector goes to receive the alms, some Arab of those who are going to pay, is employed to write a statement of the sums payable, and another collects those sums, which he hands over to the collector: thus they endeavour to prevent peculation. The collector then gives a receipt to the district or tribe for the amount that has been paid.

The Bedouins must pay this tribute immediately after the first spring month, when the camel and sheep have produced their young. The collector and the sheikh agree in appointing a certain spot, some watering-place, where all the Arabs of the tribe are directed to repair. Thus in the year 1812, Saoud collected tribute from the Bedouins about Baghdad at the watering-place called Hindye, two or three days' journey distant from that town. In the same year, the Djelás Arabs paid their tribute at a watering place twelve hours' distant from Aleppo.

Out of his private treasury, Saoud pays the expenses of his establishment and of his life-guard.

It cannot be denied, that the Wahaby chief shows great avidity in dealing with his subjects; his income is much more than sufficient to defray the public expenditure, which is not considerable, as his army costs him nothing. The Arabs complain, that if a man has a fine mare, Saoud will find out some charge of misconduct to justify him in taking the mare as a fine. The great riches that he has accumulated have increased his desire of more: and the Arabs declare that since the taking of Imám Hosseyn, where much booty was obtained, and the sacking of the Yemen towns, the character of Saoud has suffered considerable deterioration, and he has become daily more avaricious. I have not heard, however, a single instance of his depriving the meanest Arab of his property without a legal cause. The avarice of Saoud had alienated the sheikhs from his interests, long before Mohammed Aly attacked Hedjaz; and if Saoud had, on that occasion, behaved as prudently as the Pasha, in distributing money among the sheikhs, Mohammed Aly would have found it impossible to gain any firm footing in that country.

Saoud did not deny, that he had been guilty of injustice in punishing culprits too severely; and he was often heard to say, that were it not for his own and his friends' evil doings, their religion would long since have found its way to Cairo and Constantinople.

Many exaggerated statements have been made respecting the Wahaby revenue. Some well-informed Mekkans, who enjoyed frequent access to the person of Saoud and to his family, and had the best opportunities of knowing the truth and no reason for concealing it, told me, that the greatest amount ever received by Saoud into his own, or the public treasury of Derayeh, in one year, was two millions of dollars; but that in general it did not exceed one million of dollars annually. This does not include the sums received by the treasuries in the districts and towns; which, however, are generally expended, leaving no surplus at the end of the year.

His private expenses being very moderate, the chief may be supposed extremely rich in cash, which he has secreted in his mansion at Derayeh. Yet with so much wealth and power, neither Saoud nor his father were able to subjugate the free-born Arabs; they were forced to leave them in possession of their individual liberty; nor is it to be presumed, that the Arabs will ever submit to any more absolute master, and still less to a foreign invader, who may, perhaps, pass rapidly through their country, but can never bind them in lasting chains. At present their obedience is rather to the law than to Saoud, who is, in fact, but the great sheikh, not the master of Arabia; and however they may dislike the exacted tribute, they know that much of it is expended for purposes connected with their own interests: a consolation which the peasants in Turkey can never enjoy.

Military Affairs of the Wahabys.

Between the Wahabys and the Bedouins there is but little difference in military matters. Without any standing army the sheikh of a tribe collects the warlike Arabs of his camp for an excursion against the enemy, and the corps is dissolved again as soon as they return. Such is also the case with the Wahabys. Except a few hundred chosen men kept at Derayeh, neither Saoud nor his father had ever any regular army or body of troops. If the chief meditates an attack, he orders the sheikh of tribes and of districts to be on a fixed day at some certain spot, generally a well in the Desert. Sometimes the chief asks a certain number of soldiers from the sheikh, who then levies them by a kind of conscription from every village and camp under his control. Thus, if one thousand men be required from the sheikh of Kasym, every town of that province is obliged to contribute in proportion to its population. The inhabitants of towns (or in camps the Bedouins) then settle the matter amicably among themselves. All those who possess *delouls*, or camels fit for the saddle, divide into two bodies; one set goes to the war now, the other on the next summons. All from the age of eighteen to sixty must attend, whether married or unmarried, or fathers of families. All who possess mares must join the party on every summons, unless it be spcified in such summons that cavalry is not required; if a man abscond, the chief takes away his mare, or camel, or some sheep, as a fine. Saoud was very severe in the exaction of these fines; and the heavy military duties imposed on those possessing horses induced them to sell those valuable creatures, and thus reduced considerably their number in the territories under his dominion.

A general requisition for troops was sometimes made without any mention of the numbers: in this case, all who possessed a deloul were obliged to attend. On some occasions the chief merely said, "We shall not count those who join the army, but those who stay behind:" every man, therefore, capable of bearing arms, felt himself obliged to go, the poor being furnished by the rich with camels and weapons, or by the Beit el Mál. When a very distant expedition was proposed (as that against Damascus in 1810, or against Oman), Saoud commanded his chiefs to attend him with the *Sylle* only (that is, the most select horsemen and camel-riders). In that case, not more than one out of twenty joined the army. But, on all occasions, some Arabs contrive to abscond, or evade the conscription, although they know the certainty of incurring a heavy fine. This they prefer to the great expense of equipping themselves for the expedition, and providing a stock of food for forty or fifty days, each from his own purse.

One hundred pounds weight of flour, fifty or sixty pounds of dates, twenty pounds of butter, a sack of wheat or barley for the camel, and a water-skin, are the provisions of a Wahaby soldier. Dates mixed with flour, kneaded into a cake, and baked in ashes, form the morning and evening meals. The price of those provisions, the time spent on the expedition, which might be employed more profitably, the injury done to the camel by forced exertions (which kill many on the road); all these considerations render the military attendance very irksome to a poor Arab. If the summons, however, be not general, a man may hire a substitute, allowing him from eight to ten Spanish dollars for an ordinary expedition of about forty days, besides his provisions.

If camels are scarce, a man mounted upon one takes a companion (*meradíf*) behind him.

A statement formerly made, respecting

some landed properties held in bail, under obligation of military attendance, I now find to have been erroneous. All the male Wahabys are so far soldiers, that the great chief may call upon them to serve at any moment; and thus, at a fortnight's notice, assemble an army of excellent troops. But this system, though favourable to rapid movements towards an enemy's territory, or against invasion, does not suit a project of distant and permanent conquest.

The Wahaby religion prescribes continual war against all who have not adopted the reformed doctrine. As nearly the whole extent of Arabia had been reduced to submission by the Wahabys, their expeditions were chiefly directed towards their northern neighbours, from Basra, along the Euphrates, to Syria. It does not appear that they ever wished to extend their dominions beyond the limits of Arabia: so that they only attacked Irak, Mesopotamia, and Syria, for the sake of plunder. Sudden invasions were the most favourable to such an object; and no other kind of warfare has ever been practised by the Wahabys. Their chief undoubtedly wished to render himself sole master of all Arabia and its tribes; and those who rejected his invitation to become true Moslims, were exposed on all sides to attacks from his people, who damaged their fields and date-trees, or carried off their cattle; while their neighbours, who had embraced the new faith, continued unmolested by the Wahabys. Multitudes, therefore, affected to conform, that they might save their property and themselves from constant annoyance; but few provinces, or tribes, that had been outwardly converted, felt any real interest in the Wahaby cause. Many leagues were formed with the Sherif of Mekka for resisting the power of Saoud's family; and the Bedouins at first considered their subjection as they would an alliance with a stronger neighbouring tribe, which they might dissolve at any hour, and convert into a war. Provinces, strong by position and population, such as the mountains of Shammar, Hedjaz, and Yemen, and others distant from the chief seat of Wahaby power in Nedjd, soon became relaxed in their obedience to the great chief's orders, and irregular in the payment of tribute. At first, he reminded them of their duty by a parental exhortation, which they regarded as a proof of weakness, and then proceeded to open rebellion. In this case, the chief informs all his sheikhs, that "such Arabs have become enemies; and that without his further orders, every person is at liberty to attack them." He then sends three or four flying expeditions against them; and they are soon reduced to obedience, by the fear of losing their crops and their cattle. Saoud was often heard to say, that no Arabs had ever been staunch Wahabys until they had suffered two or three times from the plundering of his troops.

Some very strong and distant tribes have, however, successfully resisted the payment of tribute, although, in other respects, they profess themselves Wahabys. Thus in 1810, when Saoud's power was unshaken in Arabia, the northern Aenezes refused to pay tribute; and the chief did not think it prudent to attempt the subjection of them by main force, but continued to correspond with their sheikhs, who paid him a nominal obedience, but acted according to the interests of their own tribes, whenever they came in contact with partisans of the Wahabys.

It will be easily perceived, that the Wahabys are generally in a state of warfare. Saoud's constant practice was to make every year two or three grand expeditions. The neighbourhood of Basra (being rich in cattle and dates), and the banks of the Shat el Arab, and of the Euphrates, up to Anah, were the scenes of his annual attacks. His troops even forded the Euphrates, and spread terror in Mesopotamia, and, on the southern side of his dominions, the still unconquered provinces of Yemen, Hadramaut, and Omán, presented fertile fields of booty. Saoud did not always accompany these expeditions himself, but sent one of his sons as commander, or some distinguished sheikh; and we have even seen his black slave, Hark (حرك), at the head of several Wahaby corps.

When the Chief plans an expedition, the object of it is known to himself alone. He assembles his emírs at a certain watering-place, which is always selected in such a manner as to deceive the enemy whom he designs to attack. Thus if the expedition be intended for the northward of Derayeh, his army is assembled at a place many days' journies distant southward of Derayeh. He then actually sets out in a southern direction, but soon wheels about, and by forced marches falls upon the enemy, who is generally taken by surprise. This stratagem is very necessary, for the news spreads like lightning through Arabia, that Saoud had summoned his troops to meet at a certain spot; and if from the position of that spot any conjecture might be formed of the intended object of attack, the enemy would have time to prepare for resistance, or to fly.

The expeditions of Saoud were planned with much prudence and foresight, and executed with such celerity, that they seldom failed. Thus, when he invaded the Hauran plains in 1810, although it required thirty-five days to arrive at the point of attack, yet the news of his approach only preceded his arrival by two days; nor was it known what part of Syria he meant to attack; and thirty-five villages of Hauran were sacked by his soldiers before the Pasha of Damascus could make any demonstrations of defence.

Of the bravest and most renowned warriors among his Arabs, Saoud has formed a body-guard (*mendjyeh*), which he keeps constantly at Derayeh, and which are the only standing troops of his army. Whenever he hears of any distinguished horseman, he invites him to Derayeh, and engages him in his service, by agreeing to furnish him and his family with an annual provision of corn, butter, and dates. He gives to the man also a mare, or a good *deloul* camel. This guard constantly attends the chief on his expeditions. The name of this body-guard is dreaded by all enemies of the Wahabys, for they have never forfeited their high character for bravery. Saoud always kept them as a kind of reserve in battle, detaching small parties of them in support of his other troops. They amount to about three hundred in number, and for the greater part they fight in complete armour. Their horses are covered by the *lebs*, (a sort of quilted woollen stuff, impenetrable to lances or swords). As their service is quite voluntary, Saoud always placed great confidence in this body-guard.

Besides the *mendjyeh,* or body-guard, Saoud took with him to Derayeh many of the *agyds,* or war-chiefs of Bedouin tribes (mentioned in another place, see page 168). He lessened the power of these tribes, in carrying off their chiefs, and strengthened his own party by the accession of those renowned men; to whom, if he saw them sincerely attached to his interests, he often entrusted the direction of his expeditions.

The Wahabys make their attacks in every month of the year, even in the holy month of Ramadhán. Saoud has always shown a great predilection for the month *Zul hadje,* and his adherents pretend that he never was defeated in any expedition undertaken during that month. As Saoud, in the time of his prosperity, performed annually the pilgrimage, his enemies, especially the strong Arabian tribes of Mesopotamia, always took the opportunity of his absence at Mekka to make inroads on his territory.

If Saoud was embarrassed respecting the

choice of two measures which seemed equally advantageous, he often resorted to the practice recommended by Mohammed, which is, to address a short prayer to the Almighty before going to sleep, and to interpret the next morning whatever dream they might have had either for or against the measure. He seldom allowed the sheikhs to know any thing of his plans.

On the march every emír or sheikh has his standard. Saoud himself has several of different colours. His tents are very handsome, made at Damascus and Baghdad; but his people have only the common black Arab tents, and most of them have not any tents. Saoud's provision and baggage are carried upon two hundred camels. He takes a considerable supply on distant expeditions, that he may be able to relieve those of his troops who lose their own; and whenever he passes through any district inhabited by settlers or Bedouins, it is expected that he should treat all arriving guests in the same manner as he does at Derayeh. If the army marches at night, the chief and all the great sheikhs have torches carried before them. Night marches are only practised when the point of attack is fixed, and a space of four or five days is traversed in two. The Wahaby army is always preceded by a van-guard of thirty or forty horsemen (called *el Sabr*). They generally go before, a march of one day or perhaps of two days. The Bedouins have a similar custom of sending on a van-guard some hours in advance.

Approaching an enemy, the army always divides into three or four corps, one behind another. The first which attacks is composed of horsemen, as being the principal strength of the army. They are supported by the second line, consisting of camel-riders, who advance if the horsemen should be routed. Saoud for a long time had ceased to fight in person, and remained in the rear. The superiority of his troops over the enemy's, generally enabled him to send fresh reinforcements to his people engaged in battle, and the victory was seldom disputed for any length of time. It was a favourite stratagem of Saoud to fly before the enemy, and rallying suddenly, to fall with his chosen horsemen upon the fatigued pursuers.

To all his troops who die fighting, Saoud insures the enjoyment of paradise, according to the doctrine of the Korán. Whenever a sheikh is killed in battle, and his mare (as generally happens) gallops back towards the ranks of the troops, which she knows, the report of his death is made to the chief as tidings of glad import; because the sheikh has certainly gone to paradise. On this occasion the expression is, " Joy to you, O Saoud! the mare of such a man is come back!"

Whenever the flying corps of Wahabys plunder an encampment of Arabs, the women are obliged to strip themselves naked, while the Wahabys turn away and throw them some rags for the sake of decency. No further insult is ever offered to a female. When the plundering has ceased, the commanding emír distributes some clothes amongst them, and gives to every family a camel and sufficient provision for their journey to some camp of relations or friends. As their husbands may have been killed, or escaped by flight, it sometimes happens that women belonging to plundered camps remain during several days with the plunderers, and march in their company for the sake of being protected on the road.

In propagating their creed, the Wahabys have established it as a fundamental rule to kill all their enemies found in arms, whether they be foreign heretics (such as Syrian, Mesopotamian, or Egyptian soldiers or settlers), or Arabs themselves, who have opposed the great chief, or rebelled against him. It is this practice (imitated from the first propagators of Islám) which makes the Wahaby name so dreaded. During their four years' warfare with the soldiers of Mohammed Aly Pasha, not a single instance is recorded of their having ever given quarter to a Turk. When Kerbela (or Meshed Hosseyn) and Tayf were taken, the whole male population was massacred; and in the former town the *Haret el Abasieh*, or quarter of the Abasides, was only spared because Saoud had a particular veneration for the memory of the Abaside khalifahs. Whenever Bedouin camps are attacked, the same circumstance occurs; all who are taken with arms are unmercifully put to death. This savage custom has inspired the Wahabys with a ferocious fanaticism that makes them dreadful to their adversaries, and thus has contributed to facilitate the propagation of their faith.

But the Wahaby chief is easily induced to grant safe conduct to his enemies if they voluntarily surrender; and to this they are often inclined, as it was never known that the chief on any occasion had broken his word. Here the good faith of Bedouins towards an enemy may be recognised; a noble trait in their character. The reputation of Saoud for strict observance of a promise is allowed by his bitterest enemies, and particularly celebrated by his friends since the war with Mohammed Aly Pasha, as contrasted with the treachery of the Turks.

If the threatened Arabs surrender to Saoud before his vengeance can reach them, he usually gives to them the "*Amán ullah,*" or "God's security," with the condition of the "*halka,*" which excludes from the safe conduct all horses, camels, shields, matchlocks, lances, and swords, and all copper vessels, which must be given up as booty to the

Wahabys; the rest of their property remains untouched with the owners.

Sometimes the *Amán* is given unconditionally, and then extends over persons as well as property. All commanders of Wahaby troops have strict orders to accept any offer of submission from an enemy, and to observe inviolably the promised "Amán."

Having subdued a rebellious tribe, or province, Saoud always sent (soon after peace was concluded) for the sheikhs of the rebels, and established them with his own family at Derayeh, or in some neighbouring district, furnishing them amply with provisions. Thus he weakened their influence among their own people; replacing them by chiefs on whose attachment he could depend, chosen from those powerful families which had formerly been at variance with the sheikhs of the subdued parties. Great numbers of chiefs from all parts of Arabia are thus assembled at Derayeh and in Nedjd. They are not, by any means, close prisoners; but cannot escape from the district assigned to them. An Arab sheikh is so well known to all inhabitants of the Desert, that he can scarcely hope to remain "incognito" for any length of time.

After the taking of Medinah, Saoud found it necessary to keep there a constant garrison of Wahabys; no other instance of that kind occurred during his government. For he never thought it advisable to garrison any district that he had subdued, but relied upon the sheikh whom he had placed over it, and the dread of his own name, to keep the vanquished in subjection. Yet he commanded his new sheikhs in some districts south of Mekka to build small castles, or towers, for the defence of their residences. At Medinah, an important hold, where he knew that the people were hostile to his religion and his person, he kept a garrison of Arabs from Nedjd and Yemen armed with matchlocks, paying to each man seven dollars every month, besides rations of flour and butter. These, inhabitants of the towns of Nedjd, who are all furnished with matchlocks, form the most select corps of the Wahaby army. To them are entrusted the most difficult enterprises. It was these troops that stormed the town of Kerbelá.

Ghâleb, Sherif of Mekka, and the Turkish Pasha of Baghdád, at war with the Wahábys.—The holy cities, Mekka and Medinah, taken by the Wahábys.

During my residence in Arabia I made repeated inquiries after a written history of the Wahabys, thinking it probable that some learned man of Mekka or Medinah might have composed such a work; but my search proved fruitless. Nobody takes notes of daily occurrences, and the dates of them are soon forgotten. Some few persons, well informed of what has passed in their own neighbourhood, know but little of distant transactions; and before a complete and satisfactory account of the Wahaby affairs could be compiled, it would be necessary to make a journey through every part of Arabia. Baghdad, from its vicinity to Nedjd, the centre of the

Wahaby dominion, is, under present circumstances, the place where probably the most accurate statements might be collected.

I shall here give but few details respecting the history of this extraordinary people before the Turks re-conquered Hedjáz; an event which I can describe with more accuracy, having myself resided in that country while the war still continued.

The Wahabys had for nearly thirty years established their doctrines, made numerous proselytes, and successively conquered Nedjd and subdued most of the great Bedouin tribes, who feed their cattle there in spring and retreat afterwards to the Desert. Yet war had not been declared, nor did the Wahabys encroach upon the rights of the two governments nearest to them; that of Baghdad on the north, and that of Hedjaz towards the south. The pilgrim-caravans passed from Damascus and from Baghdad without any molestation through their territory. Their increase of power, and the assiduity with which they propagated their doctrines, seem first to have excited the jealousy of Sheríf Ghâleb. Under his authority, and partly under his influence, were placed all the tribes settled in Hedjaz, and several on the frontiers of that country. The attempts made by Abd el Azyz to gain over these latter to his party after he had subjugated their neighbours, could not be viewed with indifference by Ghâleb, whom we may consider rather as a powerful Bedouin sheikh than an eastern prince; and the same causes that produce constant wars between all great neighbouring tribes of the Desert, sowed the seeds of contest between him and the Wahabys. A few years after his succession to the government of Mekka, Ghâleb first engaged in open hostility with the Wahabys, about the year 1792 or 1793. This warfare he continued until the final surrender of Mekka. His party was then strengthened by the southern tribes of Begoum (at Taraba), Beni Salem (at Beishe), Ghâmed (in Zohrán), and the numerous Bedouins bordering on Tayf. These wars were carried on in the Bedouin style, interrupted only by a few short-lived truces. Sudden invasions were made by both parties on their enemy's territories; and booty was taken reciprocally, without much loss or advantage. Gháleb, who was then in regular correspondence with the Porte and received every year the pilgrim caravan, left no means untried for prejudicing the Turkish government against his enemies. He represented them as infidels, and their behaviour towards the Turkish hadjys, or pilgrims, did not remove this unfavourable opinion. The Porte listened more readily to these representations as the pashas of Baghdad had made statements of a similar nature. Like the Sherif of Mekka, the Pasha of Baghdad exercises influence over numerous Bedouin tribes in his neighbourhood. Several of these were already at war with the Wahabys, whose expeditions were dreaded all along the banks of the Euphrates. The country about Basra was almost every year visited by a host of these sectaries, who slaughtered many of the Arab settlers on the southern side of the river, who were subjects of the Baghdad government.

The Persian hadjys, who went to Mekka by way of Baghdad and Derayeh, complained moreover, at their return, of the great vexations they had experienced from the Wahabys, to whose chief they were obliged to pay a capitation, or passage-toll, to a considerable amount.

To direct an attack against Derayeh, no city on the Arabian border seems so well adapted as Baghdad. The pasha of this place, however, has so few pecuniary resources, and his authority so imperfectly acknowledged even within the limits of his own province, that until the year 1797, actual hostilities could not be undertaken. An invasion of Derayeh was then planned. Soleyman Pasha was at that time governor of Baghdad, a personage distinguished for bravery, energy, equity, and those talents which are necessary to a Turkish grandee, desirous of retaining his post. His lieutenant-governor was charged with the management of the expedition which marched from Baghdad. The army consisted of four or five thousand Turkish troops, and twice that number of allied Arabs of the tribes of Dhofyr, Beni Shammar, and Montefek. Their march lay parallel with the Persian Gulf, through a desert country where wells are found at every station. It was directed, in the first instance, towards the province of El Hassa, the richest and most productive part of the Wahaby dominions.

Instead of advancing from that place at once towards Derayeh (only distant five or six days' journey), they laid siege to the fortified citadel of El Hassa, which they expected to take without difficulty. The resistance was prolonged above a month; and the arrival of a strong Wahaby force under Saoud, the son of Abd el Azyz, who remained at Derayeh, excited strong doubts of success, and the Turks resolved to retreat. Saoud anticipated this measure, and, starting before them, encamped with his troops at one of the wells called *Thádj*, at the distance of three days from El Hassa. The other well of that watering-place, about two miles further off, he rendered useless by throwing into it several camel-loads of salt, which he had brought with him for that purpose. The Baghdad troops halted at this well, and it may be conceived how much both men and cattle suffered from the quality of the water; nor was it thought advisable to march, as Saoud might have fallen upon the army by surprise. On the other side, this Wahaby chief did not venture to attack the Turks, whose artillery was very formidable to him and his Arabs. Thus the two armies continued three days within sight of each other, in opposite ranks; only a single horseman from each party skirmishing occasionally in the plains between the two camps. A parley having been established, peace was concluded for six years between Saoud the Wahaby, and the pashalic of Baghdad, after which both armies returned quietly to their respective homes.

The failure of this expedition was the first cause of the misfortunes which soon after befell the Turkish party on all sides, as the Wahabys had now learned to despise the Osmanly troops. The peace was soon broken. A Persian caravan of pilgrims, escorted by a Wahaby guard, was attacked and almost totally plundered between Helle and Meshhed, by Arabs, under the Turkish jurisdiction of Baghdad. The neighbourhood of Basra was again visited by plundering parties of the Wahabys; and the sacking of Imám Hosseyn, in 1801, spread terror among all true Muselmáns, as much as it elated the sectaries. The veneration paid to that tomb of Mohammed's grandson was a sufficient cause to attract the Wahaby fury against it. Five thousand persons were massacred in the town. Old men, women, and children were spared; and the quarter called Haret el Abbasye was respected on account of the Wahaby regard for the memory of its founders. The cupola of Hosseyn's tomb was destroyed; but the treasures of that mosque, as well as those of Meshhed Aly had been secreted and afterwards removed towards Baghdad. The Wahabys, having placed trunks of palm-trees against the wall which defended the town of El Hosseyn, escaladed it, and during five or six days were engaged in the massacre and plunder of the inhabitants, after which the invaders retired and attacked the Arab settlers on the river Shat el Arab; but they were repulsed by the Zebeyr Arabs, and also by the people of Meshhed Aly. They carried off, however, all the booty previously taken, and returned to their homes.

After the plundering of Imám Hosseyn the Wahabys seem to have considerably extended their views, especially as a second expedition in the neighbourhood of Baghdad had failed. The Montefek sheikh, *Thoeny*, accompanied by his own people and the tribes of Dhofyr, Shammar, and Beni Kab, with a troop of Turkish soldiers, had marched against Nedjd. Without halting at El Hassa they passed on at once towards Derayeh, and reached the well *Szebeyhy*, distant one day's journey from the much-frequented watering-place called *el Koweyt*, within five or six days of Derayeh. While the troops were encamped there, Thoeny, the commander, was murdered by a slave belonging to Beni Khaled, a fanatic Wahaby. Saoud immediately approached, and the Baghdad soldiers fled; but several thousands of them, not knowing the roads, were slain, although most of the Bedouin troops escaped. Many of the former returned on the following night to the well of Szebeyhy that they might obtain water, hoping also either to pass unnoticed or to be treated as prisoners. But Saoud would not depart from his established custom; he ordered his Arabs to kill them all.

The Arabs of Nedjd, and of the Northern Desert, evinced more humanity than the others; they secreted in their tents many of their unfortunate enemies, gave them water for the road, and dismissed them before day-break; while, on the contrary, the southern Bedouins (principally those of Kahtan and Ateybe) unmercifully put to death all who halted at their tents. Yet even then, whatever might be their fanaticism or the commands of their chief, the Bedouins could not wholly suppress their feelings; and an eye-witness assured me that every straggler was permitted to allay his thirst before he received the mortal blow. I have already mentioned that the Wahaby chief allows no right of *dakheil*, or protection, in favour of any individual devoted to death by the Wahaby law as an enemy found in arms.

Saoud's father, Abd el Azyz, in 1801, began to attack Hedjaz and Sherif Ghaleb, with more perseverance and zeal than he had demonstrated before. Ghaleb in his campaigns against the Wahabys had been alternately victor and vanquished; he had once penetrated into Nedjd, and for a whole year kept possession of the small town called Shaara, in the province of Kasym. Another time, being surrounded by the Wahaby troops, he fought his way through them by night, and with a few followers only escaped to Beishe. The Wahabys, during some years, had extended their arms and faith among most of the mountain tribes southward of Tayf towards Yemen, people of considerable strength; and *Abou Nokta*, sheikh of Azyz was appointed commander of all. Even the Arabs near Tayf were, in 1801, obliged to yield. Ghaleb's brother-in-law, Othman el Medhayfe, a sheikh of the Adouan tribe inhabiting those parts, had been for several years at enmity with him; and as he was distinguished for all the qualities necessary to a Bedouin chief, Abd el Azyz, having subdued the country, named him chief of the tribes of Tayf and Mekka, and thence northward halfway towards Medinah. Ghaleb was now closely hemmed in, yet did not lose his energy; he collected the remainder of his faithful Arabs, and once more attempted the invasion of Nedjd, but with little success.

In 1802, Othman el Medhayfe besieged Tayf; and this pretty town, the summer residence of all the rich Mekkans and the paradise of Hedjaz, as the Arabs call it, was taken after a vigorous resistance, and shared the fate of Imám Hosseyn, with this difference, that Othman's enmity to the Sherif induced him to ruin most of the good buildings, and, in the general massacre, his soldiers were not commanded to spare either the infirm or the infants. In the course of the same year, Medhayfe also took Gonfode, a harbour on the Red Sea, seven days southward of Djidda, and belonging to the Sherif.

These successes had rendered the Wahabys very bold. Hitherto the Syrian and Egyptian caravans of pilgrims had proceeded regularly to Hedjaz, although Sherif Ghaleb had done all in his power to produce open warfare between the Porte and the Wahabys. Djezzar Pasha of Acre, while he was Pasha of Damascus, had sometimes conducted the caravan himself to Mekka in a pompous style; and so, likewise, did Abdallah, Pasha of Aden. The latter had repeatedly met at Mekka, on the plain of Arafat, during the hadj, the whole host of Wahaby pilgrims; and presents had been exchanged between him and Abd el Azyz. In refusing to let the caravans pass, the Wahabys appear to have acted from religious motives, for they knew that the soldiers who accompanied them would not attempt any hostile measures in a country where they might be at once cut off from all supplies and reinforcements. But the hadjys, or pilgrims, composing those caravans had always acted in so indecorous a manner, their chiefs had so openly sanctioned the vilest practices, and the ceremonies of the hadj itself had been so polluted by the conduct of the devotees, that the Wahabys, who had long insisted upon a reform of these disorders, resolved to terminate them. The Syrian caravan performed its pilgrimage for the last time in 1802.

In the northern parts of Hedjaz, the Wahabys attacked the strong and warlike tribe of Beni Harb, and blockaded Medinah.

In 1803 the Wahabys effected the total conquest of Hedjaz, and their power was then extended beyond all former bounds. Saoud, the son of Abd el Azyz, and Othman el Medhayfe, had collected early in that year a strong force at Tayf, and, after several battles with Sherif Gháleb, the Wahaby host approached Mekka and fixed their headquarters at the village of El Hesseynye, where the Mekkans had many pleasant summer-houses, one hour and a half distant from Mekka towards the south. Their light troops beset the town on every side; they attacked the eastern suburb called *el Moabede*, of which they kept possession for a while, together with the Sherif's palace in that quarter; from this place they made frequent irruptions into the town, which is not defended by walls. Gháleb, undismayed, bravely resisted. He laid a mine near his palace, which though not completely successful, yet obliged the enemy to retire.

They now cut off the supply of sweet water which the canal from Arafat conveys to the town, and the inhabitants were reduced to the necessity of drinking from the brackish wells. After two or three months' siege the inhabitants began to suffer extremely both from bad water and scarcity of provisions. Ghâleb himself and his soldiers had some stores at their disposal; but nothing was distributed among the lower classes, who were therefore obliged to venture out at night to collect dry grass upon the neighbouring mountains for the Sherif's horses, receiving in return a handful of corn at the Sherif's residence.

When all the cats and dogs of Mekka had been devoured, and the Sherif's provisions became scarce, he left the town with his own people, carrying off the whole of his family and baggage, having previously set fire to such furniture of his palace as was not easily portable. He retired to Djidda, and Mekka was left to its fate. On the next morning the chief inhabitants went out to capitulate, or rather, to surrender at discretion; and Saoud entered on the same day. These events occurred in April and May, 1803. The Mekkans still remember with gratitude the excellent discipline observed by these wild Wahabys on their entering the town. Not the slightest excess was committed. On the next day all the shops were opened by order of Saoud, and every article which his troops required was purchased with ready money. Saoud declared that he might have taken the town by assault long before, but that he wished to avoid disorder and excesses; and he told the olemas in full council that he had seen Mohammed in a dream, who threatened him that he should not survive three days if a single grain of corn were forcibly taken from the holy city.

The people of Mekka now became Wahabys; that is, they were obliged to pray more punctually than usual, to lay aside and conceal their fine silk dresses, and to desist from smoking in public. Heaps of Persian pipes, collected from all the houses, were burnt before Saoud's head-quarters, and the sale of tobacco was forbidden. The brother of Ghaleb, *Abd el Mayen*, was placed by Saoud at the head of the Mekkan government; and a learned man from Derayeh, called *Ibn Name*, was appointed kady of the town. So upright was this Bedouin judge that his sentences have become almost proverbial, and the Mekkans now say in derision of their venal Constantinopolitan kady "There goes Ibn Name!" At this time the prayers for the sultan, usually recited in the grand mosque, were abolished.

From Mekka Saoud turned his arms against Djidda, where Sherif Ghâleb had taken refuge. The town was besieged for eleven days, but the inhabitants fought bravely; and Saoud, despairing of being able to force the walls, retreated. Many persons affirm that Ghâleb, who had made preparations on board a large ship in the harbour, for escaping by sea, induced Saoud to retire, by a bribe of fifty thousand dollars. The Wahabys now moved back towards the Northern Desert. Ghâleb issued from Djidda, and resumed the government of Mekka (in July 1803), where the small Wahaby garrisons of the two castles capitulated, and Abd el Mayen, a man of peaceable character, again submitted to his brother; but Ghâleb himself, soon after, knowing that he could not defend the place for any time, compromised with Saoud, and surrendered to that Wahaby chief. The details of this war, although it had occurred only eleven years before my travels in Hedjaz, were related to me with different circumstances, by various persons.

Ghâleb enjoyed, on this occasion, more favourable conditions than those usually granted to other proselyte chiefs. He was left in possession of his towns and their incomes. Several Bedouin tribes were permitted to remain under his influence; and in consideration of his high station, and the respect due to those who inhabited the holy city, neither himself, nor the Mekkans, were required to pay tribute to the great chief. On the other hand, the Sherif renounced the custom duties at Djidda from all true Wahabys.

The capture of Mekka was the signal for other advantages in Hedjaz. The tribe of Harb was obliged to yield, but not without a severe contest, which so exasperated the Wahabys, that they treated them more rigorously than any other Bedouins of the country. A branch of the Harbs, called *Beni Sobh*, successfully maintained themselves in their steep mountains, and were never reduced to submission. Yembo surrendered when the Beni Harb and Djeheyny (another large tribe of that neighbourhood) had joined the Wahaby party; and Medinah soon after (early in the spring of 1804) followed its example. The principal man of this city, Hassan el Kaladjy, had usurped a despotic power, and been guilty of the greatest injustice during the general distress, while all supplies were withholden from the town by the Wahabys. He at last seized upon the treasure attached to the tomb of Mohammed, and divided part of it among his adherents; after which, he proposed to surrender. The inhabitants of Medinah who are much more inclined to the Turkish interest than the Mekkans, and live wholly upon the profits derived from those who visit their mosque, were not so leniently treated as the people of Mekka had been. The usual tribute was required, but private property was not plundered. The chief Turkish officer of the town, the Aga el Haram (appointed by the sultan), was obliged to leave Medinah, with many Turkish hadjys; and El Medheyan, whom the Wahaby chief had nominated sheikh of the whole tribe of Harb, was appointed governor of Medinah.

Here the Wahabys enforced, with great strictness, the regular observance of prayers. The names of all the adult male inhabitants were called over in the mosque after morning, mid-day, and evening prayers; and those who did not obey the call were punished. A respectable woman, accused of having smoked the Persian pipe, was placed upon a jack-ass, with the pipe suspended from her neck, round which was twisted the long flexible tube, or snake: in this state she was paraded through the town. Hassan el Kaladjy still retained some influence under the Wahabys, and continued to annoy the inhabitants.

Saoud soon after visited Medinah, and stripped Mohammed's tomb of all the valuable articles that it still possessed (the gold vessels had been previously taken away). He also endeavoured to destroy the high dome erected over the tomb, and would not allow Turkish pilgrims to approach Medinah from any quarter; and several of them, who attempted to pass from Yembo to the town, were ill treated; their beards also were cut off, as the Wahabys, who themselves have short scanty beards, declared, that the prophet did not wear so long and bushy a beard as those of the northern Turks. This was done by the low classes of Wahabys in derision of the Turks, and not in obedience to any law, or command.

The Wahabys, however, continued always to visit Medinah in honour of Mohammed; and they paid a devout visit also to the mosque of that prophet, but not, like other Muselmáns, to his tomb, situated in that mosque. The tomb was left uninjured; but Saoud regarded as idolatrous any visits, prayers, or exclamations, addressed to it, and therefore he prohibited them. But it is false to assert, as the Turks have done, that the pilgrimage to Medinah was abolished by the Wahabys.

Even before the capture of Medinah, the great pilgrimages by caravans had ceased. The Syrian caravan, commanded by Yousef Aga, an officer of Abdallah Pasha, had not been able (in 1803) to reach Medinah, but retreated when within a few hours' distance.

They were not molested on their return. The Egyptian hadj of that year did not venture to take the land route, as the tribes of Harb and Djeheyne had now become Wahabys; but the Mahmal, and a few pilgrims, went by sea to Djidda, with about four or five hundred soldiers, under the command of Sherif Pasha, whom the Porte had named governor of Djidda. The Persian hadj, too, had been kept back since 1802; and the same was the case with the Yemen caravan of pilgrims: so that, after 1803, no regular hadj caravan arrived at Mekka, where a few only succeeded in finding their way. The Mahmal was detained at Djidda, and Sherif Pasha died in 1804 in Hedjaz. It was suspected that he had been poisoned by order of Ghaleb.

Abd el Azyz survived the taking of Mekka, but did not witness that of Medinah. He was assassinated in the latter end of 1803 by a Persian, whose relations the Wahabys had murdered. Abd el Azyz was succeeded by his eldest son, Saoud, superior to his father in the necessary qualities of a religious leader of Bedouin warriors. He had for many years conducted all the wars; and to him may be ascribed the conquest of Hedjaz.

While Medinah was compelled to admit within its gates the northern Wahabys, those of the south were not idle in extending the influence of their arms. Abou Nokta, the sheikh of Asyr, had been for some time at war with the Sherif Hamoud, who at that time governed the Yemen coast from near Gonfode southward to Beit-el-Fakyh, a country which he had himself detached from the jurisdiction of his nearest relation, the Imam of Szana. Hamoud relying upon the walls of his town, and five or six hundred cavalry in his service, had always refused to adopt the Wahaby faith. Near the close of the year 1804, Abou Nokta, with a numerous body of his Arabs, descended from the mountains, and spread over the coast such multitudes of Wahabys, that Hamoud was obliged to fly The richest towns on the Yemen coast, Loheya and Hodeyda, were plundered; but Abou Nokta did not venture to remain in them long with his army; he retreated again to the mountains, thence keeping in check the whole coast of Yemen. Hamoud again declared his adherence to the new faith.

Although Hedjaz was now conquered, the Sherif's power continued to be very great. His name and venerable office; his great talents for intrigue; and his personal influence over many Bedouin tribes, that still resisted the authority of Saoud, and the valuable presents made to the latter, whenever he visited Mekka, caused the Wahaby chief to connive at several of Ghâleb's proceedings. When Saoud approached Mekka for the annual pilgrimage (which he regularly performed, with great numbers of his Arabs), a whole caravan of camels, loaded with presents from the Sherif, came to meet him at Zeyme, two days distant from the city. The presents comprised all sorts of choice provisions, clothes, and other articles, besides several camel-loads of Indian muslin, to serve for the *ihram*, or mantle, in which the pilgrims enter the sacred territory. All his officers received similar presents. The women and children had all new suits of clothes, and quantities of sweetmeats. Such, indeed, was the liberality of Ghâleb on these occasions, that Saoud often said, it made him blush, and rendered it impossible for him to treat the Sherif as he otherwise should have done.

At Mekka the power of Ghâleb was thus always balancing that of Saoud, and at Djidda the authority of the former continued in full force. A good garrison was constantly kept in that town, which the Wahaby troops never entered, although the inhabitants were obliged to profess their conversion to the new faith, whenever any of Saoud's officers visited them on business. In the course of 1805, Medhayfe, who still continued his hostility against Ghâleb, made several attempts to seize Djidda with his own Arabs, and without any formal authority from the Wahaby chief. He took possession of the wells belonging to the town; but the inhabitants, including foreigners who happened to be there, took up arms and frustrated his design.

Although the hadj caravans were now interrupted, great numbers of pilgrims flocked every year to Mekka from all parts of the Turkish empire. They came by sea to Djidda, and no orders were even given by Saoud

to prevent them from going on to Mekka.
These pilgrims of course were obliged to
comply with all the Wahaby precepts; but
those who conducted themselves accordingly,
and with decency, experienced no harsh
treatment. I knew in 1810, at Aleppo, a native
of that town, who informed me that he had
for the last six years annually performed
the pilgrimage by way of Cairo and Cosseir,
without any molestation. Pilgrims from Yemen, India, and the Negro countries arrived
as before at Djidda by sea, about the month
of the hadj; but they found it expedient to
leave their arms at Djidda, as the wearing
of any weapons at Mekka exposed foreigners
to suspicion, and often to ill-usage. The pilgrimage, therefore, was never abolished, either
with regard to Arabs or Turks; and had the
great Syrian and Egyptian caravans placed
confidence in the safe-conduct of the Wahabys, they might have crossed the Desert
with security, but without any armed force.

Hedjaz was now tranquil. The communication being opened with all the interior,
and few foreigners arriving, provisions were
abundant and cheap; but the inhabitants

of the holy cities had lost their principal means of subsistence, derived from their intercourse with foreign merchants coming to the pilgrimage.

In this state Hedjaz continued during the years 1806, 1807, and 1808. The Sherif's power was daily declining, and Saoud's authority was acknowledged over the far greater part of Arabia. In the years above mentioned, this Wahaby chief made several incursions against Basra and Mesopotamia. One of his attacks on Basra about this time proved unfortunate. His troops were engaged in plundering the villages about that town in small parties, when they were overpowered by a strong body of Kab and Montefek Arabs, and upwards of fifteen hundred of the Wahabys were slain. A Negro slave of Saoud, called *Hark*, at the head of a strong troop, made various expeditions into the Syrian Desert, and frightened the Bedouins in the very vicinity of Aleppo. The Euphrates was forded by Wahaby detachments, and the wealthy camps of the Mesopotamian tribes were attacked and plundered, even in the neighbourhood of Baghdad. In the south,

Abou Nokta continued to harass Yemen by rapid incursions and frequent plundering. Sana, however, does not seem to have been ever made the object of attack. Saoud, who knew the jealousy prevailing between Hamoud, the governor of the coast, and Abou Nokta, chief of the mountains, alternately promised to each of them the plunder of that rich city, which, from its feeble means of defence, could not have resisted a slight attack; but he never actually ordered either to undertake the conquest of it; and this, it was supposed, he wished to reserve for himself.

During those years the Porte remained almost inactive. Saoud had come to open hostilities with the Turkish government, since he forbad the people to pray in their mosques for the welfare of the Sultan, as was usually done on Fridays. This was effected by the artful contrivance of Sherif Ghálib, who wished to cause an irreconcileable rupture between Saoud and the Porte. A brave warrior, Yousef Pasha, had been placed at the head of that government; and it was expected that he could lead the pilgrim caravans by force through the Desert. But the sums destined for that caravan (which are assessed upon the income of Damascus), he applied to his own use. Nor did the Syrian Bedouins, who usually escort the caravan, show any great desire to be concerned in so hazardous an enterprise.

Yousef Pasha made, in the year 1809, some faint preparations of attack against the district of Djof, consisting of several villages on the road from Damascus to Nedjd, twelve days distant from Damascus. But it was only a vain demonstration of his zeal, and never took place. The greatest loss which the Wahabys ever experienced was, in the course of that year, the destruction of their fortified harbour on the Persian Gulf, called *Rás el Kheyme,* which was laid in ashes by an English expedition sent from Bombay; as its piratical inhabitants of the *Gowasim* or *Djowasim* tribe had committed numerous depredations upon the English commerce in that sea. A cousin of Saoud was among the killed on that occasion.

In the same year a fresh war broke out between Abou Nokta and Sherif Hamoud·

the former descended from his mountains, and encamped in front of Abou Arysh. Hamoud sallied forth at night from that town with about forty horsemen, dressed as Wahaby Bedouins, and taking a circuitous route, arrived by dawn of day in the rear of his enemies; whose camp they entered without having excited any suspicion, for they were supposed to be friendly mountaineers. But in front of Abou Nokta's tent they shouted their war-cry, and Hamoud killed that chief with his own hand as he was starting up from his mat, and was fortunate enough to escape in the general disorder.

Sheikh Tamy, of the small Refeydha tribe (belonging to Asyr), was appointed by Saoud to succeed Abou Nokta. Hamoud again submitted; but his allegiance was always doubtful, and he never was punctual in remitting the tribute.

In 1810, Saoud struck terror into the heart of Syria, by attacking the neighbourhood of Damascus with about six thousand men. His arrival was unexpected; and Yousef Pasha's army was unable to check his progress. During three days he plundered thirty-five villages in the Hauran district, only two days distant from Damascus, and burnt all the corn wherever he passed; but he was not so unmerciful to the inhabitants as he had been on other occasions; and the lives of many peasants were spared. A Christian woman, made prisoner, and carried off as a slave, was some days afterwards released by order of Saoud. He might easily have taken the town, had he known the terror inspired by his approach among the inhabitants, who began to send off all their valuable property to the mountains of Libanon; but his plan was, undoubtedly, to make frequent plundering visits; so that Damascus, at least, would have been induced to surrender voluntarily. He returned with considerable booty.

A numerous caravan of Moggrebyns, which had come by land to Cairo, performed the pilgrimage this year. On their arrival in Hedjaz, they received permission to visit Mekka, as Saoud had always declared that the Moggrebyns behaved with decency, and were religious people. He met with the leader of this caravan, a son of the Emperor of Marocco, and presents were exchanged between them.

While the Pashas of Baghdad and of Damascus had, at different times, made hostile demonstrations against the Wahabys, Egypt remained a passive spectator of the fate of Hedjaz; and the small expedition of about five hundred men, fitted out in 1804 by Sherif pasha of Djidda, was the only feeble effort made on the part of Egypt to restore the Turkish influence over the holy cities. The turbulent state of Egypt—the division of power among the numerous Beys, who acknowledged but a nominal obedience to the pasha sent by the Porte—and the desire of those Beys to possess the money appropriated for the pilgrim-caravans, and for the holy cities—all these circumstances caused every faithful Sunny to despair of ever seeing the hadj revived, as long as Egypt should remain in that condition. For all parties knew, that from Egypt only could Hedjaz be conquered. The immense Desert extending between that country and Damascus, rendered impossible the transport of sufficient provision and ammunition for a regular campaign with an enemy, whose first measure would be to cut off all other communication. A strong body of troops, accompanied by a vast number of loaded camels, might perhaps, after many serious difficulties, succeed in reaching Medinah, and even Mekka: they might also take those towns; but all the troops and camels that they could muster would not enable them to keep the whole country in subjection, to defend it against an active enemy, and to render themselves independent of foreign supplies.

This last consideration alone showed, that from Egypt all efforts must be directed for liberating the country from its Bedouin masters. Hedjaz depends almost exclusively upon Egypt for every necessary of life, which may be carried there by sea, through Yembo and Djidda, the very gates of both the holy cities, without exposing them, during their passage, to any of the casualties attending a journey of thirty or forty days, over a barren and hostile desert, from Syria to Mekka.

The Wahabys did not refuse to admit pilgrims from all quarters into the holy cities: they had often publicly offered to allow their peaceable passage should they behave with decorum, and not assume any airs of supremacy in these countries, which the natural disposition and character of their inhabitants, as well their geographical position, had made an Arabian and not a Turkish province. After Mekka and Medinah had yielded to the Wahabys, after the Sherif himself had become a proselyte to their faith, and acted in open hostility against the Porte, and all Hedjaz followed his example, the most natural measure that presented itself was to cut off any farther supplies, by shutting the ports of Cosseir and Suez against all Hedjaz shipping. That such a step was not taken during the Mammelouk reign, when no general measure could ever be carried into effect in Egypt, where, besides, those Beys whose influence predominated, derived considerable profits from the Hedjaz trade, will not surprise us. But one might reasonably wonder at the neglect of this prohibitory system, under the government of Mohammed Aly, who, since 1805, possessed the port of Suez, and since 1808 that of Cosseir; and who had promised in the strongest terms, to his sovereign, that he would rescue Hedjaz from the Wahabys.

During all that time, and even in the beginning of 1810, when Mohammed Aly made serious preparations for attacking the Wahabys, there were daily arrivals at Suez and Cosseir of ships from Djidda and Yembo, which went back loaded with corn and provisions for the Sherif, as well as for private adventurers; nor was that traffic discontinued until a few months before the sailing of the first expedition from Suez against Arabia, when fears were entertained of the ships being seized in that port for the conveyance of troops. To withhold all supplies from Hedjaz for a single year, would have produced most alarming consequences in that country, where it is not usual to lay by provisions for more than two months; and the scanty supplies brought from Nedjd and Yemen could not have prevented a famine. Had this actually occurred, the Wahaby chief would certainly have been induced to make terms with the governor of Egypt, highly in favour of the the hadj, and of the whole Turkish empire.

Although the Wahaby army occupying Hedjaz might always have been able to subsist upon supplies furnished by the interior, yet the miseries of famine in the sacred cities would have strongly affected those religious fanatics, who had frequently evinced their veneration for those places, and their regard for the inhabitants. The Sherif himself would have employed all his interest with the Wahabys (and even since his submission he possessed considerable influence) to terminate a state of things which, besides distressing his own people, (a matter perhaps of little consideration to him,) would have reduced a great part of his income, arising from trade and the duties levied upon merchandise going to Egypt, or coming from that country.

As so easy and so natural a measure was not attempted by Mohammed Aly, his partisans endeavoured to excuse his neglect by alleging that it would be a heinous sin to starve the Holy Land; but those acquainted with the pasha's character knew that such a consideration was of little weight with him, while persons conversant with the Red-Sea commerce believed that the gains which flowed into his treasury through this channel (partly by his own selling of corn and provisions at Suez and Cosseir, and partly by the custom duties,) were so considerable that he declined the execution of his sovereign's orders, which might have caused a reduction or cessation of those profits. All the nations of the Turkish empire united in execrating the Wahabys, and demanded an expedition, resembling our old crusades, against those heretics. Yet their ships were seen carrying the stores of Egypt from Suez to the barren soil of Hedjaz, thus supplying their own enemies, at the same time that caravans loaded with ammunition destined to be employed against those enemies daily arrived at Suez from Cairo.

The account of such absurd proceedings and miserable half-measures will scarcely be credited by an European reader; but a residence of some years in the Levant will prove, that whenever the smallest, or even temporary loss, is apprehended by a Turkish governor, nothing can induce him to adopt measures of general utility : his views never extend beyond the present moment, while he sacrifices the interests of his sovereign and the welfare of his subjects to any certainty of the most trifling pecuniary advantage. But his cupidity often overshoots its mark, and finally tends to his own ruin, or at least forms an impediment to his own operations.

Mohammed Aly, Pasha of Cairo, despatches his son Tousoun Pasha with a Turkish army to invade Arabia.—Thomas Keith, a Scotchman, (Ibrahím Aga,) commander of Tousoun's Mammelouks—His intrepidity—Ahmed Aga, surnamed Bonaparte—Medinah taken by the Turks, and Mekka surrendered to them.

WHEN Mohammed Aly in 1804, was appointed Pasha of Egypt, where for the last two years he had exercised all the influence which his numerous troops and his own subtlety could give him over the feeble remnant of the once formidable Mammelouks, the principal duty imposed on him by orders of the Porte was to attempt the reconquest of the holy cities. He was aware that to disobey these orders would be punished with removal from the government; and the Porte, to stimulate his exertions, promised him the pashalik of Damascus for one of his sons, as soon as he should obtain possession of Mekka and Medinah; his own ambition also made that object highly desirable, as the deliverance of the holy cities would exalt him far above all other pashas of the Turkish empire, and add such celebrity to his name that the Porte might never afterwards be induced to oppose his interests. During the first years of his government, the pasha was constantly engaged in skirmishes with the Mammelouks; and it was not until 1810 that he came to a compromise, which made them abandon their pretensions upon all Lower and the greater part of Upper Egypt, engaged them to re-enter Cairo under a promise of safe-conduct, and caused the treacherous massacre of them soon after in the castle of that city.

Near the end of 1809 Mohammed Aly began seriously to prepare for his expedition. It was above all things necessary to have a sufficient number of ships at his command for the transport of troops and provisions.

If he had seized upon a single *dow*, coming from Hedjaz, all others would have been frightened away, and an injury done to his undertaking. He, therefore, resolved to construct a flotilla, and during 1809, 1810, and in the beginning of 1811, twenty-eight large and small vessels (from one hundred to two hundred and fifty tons burden) were built at Suez, where about one thousand workmen, among whom were Greeks and other Europeans, found constant employment. The wood prepared at Boulak, near Cairo, was carried upon camels across the Desert, and large magazines of corn, biscuit, and other provisions, were about the same time formed at Suez. As it was not easy to transport in such vessels numerous bodies of cavalry across a dangerous sea, it was necessary to provide for their passage by land. The castles on the hadj road, between Cairo and Yembo, (Adjeroud, Nakhel, Akaba, Moeyleh, and el Wodj,) were all repaired and strengthened by new walls, and garrisoned principally with Moggrebyn foot-soldiers, well accustomed to treat with Bedouins, and those living in the vicinity of the castles were engaged by presents to go with their camels and bring back from Cairo provisions, which were to be placed in the store-rooms of those castles.

At the same time magazines of grain were established at Cosseir; but this port had not, in the beginning of the war, that importance which it afterwards acquired as the exclusive depôt of provisions, being considerably nearer to Hedjaz than Suez, which continued to be merely the mercantile port of Cairo.

When Ghâleb, the Sherif of Mekka, heard that such considerable preparations were made for the invasion of Hedjaz, and that Mohammed Aly possessed greater resources than any other pasha who attempted to force an entrance into that country, he thought it advisable to commence a secret correspondence with him, and to affirm that although irresistible circumstances had obliged him to adopt Wahabyism, yet he was ready to throw off the yoke at the first appearance of a respectable Turkish army on the shore of Hedjaz. In the course of this correspondence he added much information respecting the actual state and force of the Wahabys, the disposition of the Hedjaz Bedouins, and the best mode of attack.

To the first merchant of Cairo, *Seyd Mohammed el Mahrouky*, who had himself often been at Mekka and was deeply concerned in the Red Sea trade, were entrusted by Mohammed Aly the political conduct of the war, and all the necessary arrangement with the Bedouins of the Red Sea: and it cannot be doubted that he had a considerable share in the final success of this enterprise. Mohammed Aly was of too suspicious a character to place much confidence in the assurances of Ghaleb, whose artful and wily talents were well known; but it became necessary to soothe the apprehensions that Ghaleb might entertain of a foreign invader. The fairest promises were made to him, that his authority in Hedjaz should be respected; that the custom duties of Djidda (the chief source of his revenue) should be left in his hands; and the soldiers destined to embark on the expedition were encouraged by reports secretly spread, that Sherif Ghaleb, with all his force, would join them on their arrival.

The state of Egypt was not yet sufficiently

tranquil to allow the absence of Mohammed Aly himself. In the southern part of Upper Egypt the Mammelouks still continued a teasing warfare with the pasha's troops. Tousoun Bey, the second son of Mohammed Aly, a youth of eighteen years, was placed in command of the first expedition against the Wahabys, which after much delay was ready for departure at the end of August, 1811. Tousoun Bey, while yet a mere boy, had given proofs of extraordinary courage in the Mammelouk war; and courage being so rare a quality among the present race of degenerate Osmanlys, and still more rare in the family of a pasha, his friends reckoned him competent to the most arduous undertaking. Ahmed Aga, the treasurer, or kheznedar, of Mohammed Aly, was sent with Tousoun as a commander of equal bravery and graver counsel. His butchering achievements in the wars against the Mammelouks and the Arabs in Egypt, had exalted him in the eyes of his master; his utter disregard of human life, his contempt of all moral principles, and his idle boasting had procured him the surname of *Bonaparte*, which afforded him much delight, and by which he was universally designated in Egypt.*

That he was a brave soldier cannot be denied; but drunkenness and lusts of the vilest kind had deprived his mind of all energy and judgment.

To these two commanders was joined El Mahrouky, above mentioned, whose department was the diplomatic negotiation with the Sherif and the Bedouins. Two great olemas of Cairo, Sheikh el Mehdy and Sheikh el Tahtawy, likewise embarked with the troops; that by their controversial learning, as it was said, they might convince the Wahabys of the errors which they had adopted in their new faith. The expedition consisted of two parts. The infantry, composed principally of Arnaut soldiers amounting to fifteen hundred or two thousand effective men, under Saleh Aga and Omar Aga, embarked at Suez for Yembo, and took with them all the new-built ships carrying provisions. The cavalry, with

* I have in my possession some original letters addressed to him by the Wahaby chief, in which he is styled "*Ahmed Aga Bonaparte.*"

Tousoun Bey and Ahmed Bonaparte, forming a body of about eight hundred men, Turkish horsemen and armed Bedouins (under the command of Shedíd, sheikh of the Howeytát tribe) proceeded by land.

In October 1811, the fleet arrived near Yembo, the troops landed at a short distance from the town, of which they took possession, after a feeble resistance of two days, by capitulation. A fortnight afterwards, the cavalry arrived by land, not having met with any opposition from the Bedouin tribes, who had already been conciliated by considerable sums of money. The taking of Yembo was proclaimed as a first victory over the Wahabys, and a favourable omen for the future success of the expedition. The troops remained several months inactive; the infantry at Yembo, the sea-port; and the cavalry, with the Bedouins, at Yembo el Nakhel, distant from the sea-port six hours, and the chief station of the Djeheyne Arabs. This time was consumed in negotiations. Tousoun Bey found that Hedjaz was not by any means in such a state as he had expected from the representations which Sherif Ghaleb had made. The Bedouin inhabitants of that country, and especially the two great tribes of Harb and Djeheyne, whatever might be their dislike of the Wahabys, and their desire to participate again in the rich tribute and gains arising from the Turkish pilgrim caravan, were completely overawed by the power and vigilance of Saoud, the Wahaby chief; and they did not dare to stir as long as the Turks continued without some decided advantage, which might give them hopes of ultimate success in joining their party. The taking of Yembo alone could not be reckoned of much importance in the prosecution of the war, although it was highly useful for the Turks to have a safe place of anchorage for their vessels and a depôt for their stores.

At the time when the Turkish expedition arrived, Yembo was not garrisoned by Wahabys; but the Sherif Ghaleb kept in it a governor and about one hundred soldiers. These had attempted some resistance; but the inhabitants obliged them to retreat, fearing that the town might be exposed to the assault of savage troops, and thinking it prudent to capitulate. The Sherif remained a quiet spectator of this commencement of war; he wrote letters to Tousoun Bey, in which he excused himself for not joining him on account of the smallness of his force and his dread of the Wahabys; but he again solemnly declared that he would throw off the mask, and openly attack the latter as soon as the Turks should gain any important advantage, which might at once bring over to their side all the Bedouins of Hedjaz. Meanwhile he strongly garrisoned Djidda and Mekka, and, when urged by Saoud to join him against the invaders, excused himself by expressing his fears of a sudden maritime attack on Djidda, which might lead to the capture of the more distant Mekka.

It was evidently the Sherif's plan either to temporise and to fall upon whichever party should suffer the first signal defeat, or to wait until the two parties were weakened by the war and then to drive them both out of his dominions. The only Hedjaz Bedouins whom Tousoun Bey was able to detach from the Wahabys, were a few branches of the Djeheyne, inhabiting the neighbourhood of

Yembo, while the greater part of that tribe and the whole of the Harbs, who bordered upon their territories, remained insensible to his offers.

It became necessary, however, to begin a campaign, lest the people of Hedjaz, as well as the enemy, should regard inactivity as the result of fear, and negotiation as a proof of weakness. To march towards Mekka or Djidda would have obliged the Sherif who occupied those towns to declare himself at once decidedly for one party or the other. A decision which Tousoun Bey had more to dread than the Wahabys. He, therefore, wisely directed his views towards Medinah (six days distant from Yembo). Medinah was always considered the best walled town of Hedjaz, the rampart of that province against Nedjd, and the strong-hold of the Wahabys: the possession of it, therefore, might open or obstruct the passage of the Syrian hadj. The taking of Medinah would induce a number of Bedouins to join the army; and Sherif Ghaleb, when he learned that such was the design, formally promised to declare against Saoud whenever that event should take place.

Having left a garrison at Yembo, Tousoun Bey advanced with his troops in January, 1812, towards Medinah. After a slight skirmish he entered Beder, a small town two days distant from Yembo, and occupied by the tribe of Harb. Beder is situated at the entrance of those mountains which it was necessary to cross on the way to Medinah. Some resistance was expected from the Beni Harb, who held the passes through those mountains; but nothing was known of the presence of any Wahaby troops. Tousoun left a small garrison at Beder, and proceeded with his army to Szafra, a market-place of the Harb tribe (eight hours from Beder); there, after some short fighting, a body of that tribe, gave way. At four hours from Szafra, the road leads through a narrow passage (from forty to sixty yards across), between steep and rugged mountains, at the entrance of which, the village of Djedeyde is situated, among groves of palm-trees, the principal settlement of the Beni Harb; to whom, in former times, the Syrian pilgrim-caravan had often been obliged to pay considerable sums for the permission of passing unmolested.

In this defile, which extends lengthways about one hour and a half, the Turkish army was at once assailed by the united force of the tribe of Harb. After some skirmishing, the Turks, believing that they had obtained the advantage, were induced to pursue the Arabs into the very middle of that pass; when, on a sudden, the mountains, on both sides, were thickly covered with the Wahaby troops, who had arrived the day before from Nedjd, and of whom the Turks had not the slightest information. The Wahabys were commanded by Abdallah and Faysal, the sons of Saoud, and their number amounted to twenty thousand infantry and camel-riders, and from six to eight hundred horsemen. By retreating into the village of Djedeyde, and fortifying themselves there, the Turks might have withstood the attack, and obtained an honourable capitulation, as the number of the enemy rendered it impossible for them to remain long upon the same spot.

On the first cry of alarm, however, the Turkish infantry fell back, and the cavalry, ordered to cover their retreat, soon joined in the flight; while their nimble enemies, pressing them from behind, and outrunning them along the mountain side, poured incessant vollies upon them. Under such desperate circumstances, Tousoun Pasha did not forfeit his reputation for bravery, and acted as became the honour of a commander. Accompanied at first by two horsemen only of his own suite, after vain endeavours to rally his troops, he hastened to the rear, and plunged into the enemy's ranks, to make them desist from the pursuit.

Persons who were present assured me, that while tears gushed from his eyes, Tousoun exclaimed to the fugitive Turks, "Will none of you stand by me?" About twenty horsemen at last joined him; when luckily the Wahabys were, for a short time, engaged in seizing the baggage of the army, and this circumstance caused them to slacken their pursuit; and when the Turks had regained the open space beyond the entrance of the defile, their cavalry rallied, and in some degree protected the others. Had the Wahabys eagerly pushed forward over the mountains, the whole body of Turks would have been annihilated: they contented themselves, however, with taking all the Turkish baggage, four field-pieces, almost every one of their camels, and much booty, which they found in the girdles of the Arnauts, who had enriched themselves with the Mammelouks' spoils in Egypt. About twelve hundred were killed on that day Tousoun Bey retreated to Beder, set the camp there on fire, not having any means of removing it, and abandoning, for the same reason, his military chest, returned to the sea-shore nearest to Beder, where several of his ships lay at anchor, in a bay called Bereyka. Here he embarked with very few attendants, and proceeded to Yembo by sea. The rest of his troops arrived some days after in great distress; but fortunately for them, the Wahabys, imagining that a strong Turkish corps was intrenched at Beder, did not immediately pursue their success; and thus all who were sufficiently strong to perform the journey, finally reached Yembo.

When the Wahabys knew that their enemies had secured themselves in Yembo, they sent out parties of troops to scour the country up to the very walls of that town. The Sherif, immediately after he received intelligence, that the Turkish expedition had failed, joined the Wahabys in person at Beder. It was at first proposed to storm Yembo; but this project was abandoned, from fear of the Arab inhabitants, who, no doubt, would fight with desperation, as they had espoused the Turkish interests with cordiality. The Wahabys found it unnecessary to blockade the town any longer, and retreated to the interior, ready to assemble again at a moment's notice, whenever the Turks should venture a second time to lead an army into the open country. On this retreat, they left the Harb Bedouins to harass the Turks, and cut off all supplies from the town.

Reverting to the account of those dangerous circumstances in which Tousoun Pasha was placed, when all his people had forsaken him except two horsemen, I must here record an anecdote respecting one of those brave soldiers, called Ibrahím Aga, acting as chief of Tousoun's Mammelouks (Anakder Agassy). This was a young man of about twenty years, a native of Edinburgh, named Thomas Keith. Having been taken prisoner at the last English expedition against Egypt, together with many others of his regiment, (the 72nd Highlanders,) in which he served as gunsmith, he became a Muselmán, and was purchased from the soldier who had made him prisoner, by Ahmed Bonaparte above mentioned. A favourite Sicilian Mammelouk of his master having insulted the young Scotchman, blows ensued; swords were drawn, and the Sicilian fell. Ibrahím Aga escaped from the wrath of Ahmed Bonaparte, and implored the protection of Mohammed Aly's lady, who befriended him and caused her son, Tousoun Bey, to engage him in his service. Tousoun, in one of those capricious fits of ill-humour to which Turkish despots are so often subject, gave orders that the young Scotchman should be put to death for some trifling neglect of duty; but the brave fellow with his sword defended the entrance of his room for half an hour against several assailants, then threw himself out of the window, and again escaped to his kind protectress, who soon reconciled him with his master. Tousoun Bey at length became sensible of Ibrahim's merit as a courageous soldier, made him chief of his Mammelouks, and, after his valorous conduct at Djedeyde, promoted him to the office of treasurer, the second post in rank at the court of a Pasha. He again fought bravely at Medinah and at Taraba (hereafter mentioned), was appointed governor of Medinah in April 1815, and two months after, when hastening with two hundred and fifty horsemen to the assistance of Tousoun Bey (encamped in the province of Kasym), was overtaken by a superior number of Wahabys, and shared the fate of his troops, who were all destroyed. In this last action the gallant Scotchman killed four Wahabys with his own hand; and Abdallah Ibn Saoud confessed, that Tousoun Bey and his faithful treasurer were the two bravest men of the Turkish army.

The losses which they had sustained, now completely disheartened the troops. Saleh Aga and Omar Aga, the two chiefs of infantry, both declared that they could not fight any longer in Hedjaz. Tousoun Bey therefore resolved to send them back: they returned to Cosseir, and, on their voyage to Cairo, recruited their corps with a number of individuals discontented with the Pasha. Having approached that city, they assumed such an imposing attitude, that Mohammed Aly found it necessary to exert all his art in inducing them by threats, as well as by presents, to quit Egypt. Both had formerly pillaged the richest districts of Upper Egypt, and embarked at Alexandria with considerable treasures.

The troops of Tousoun Bey had been much reduced in horses by the fatiguing land journey even before their arrival at Yembo, and they were forsaken by most of the Bedouin horsemen who had accompanied them. About two hundred horses were killed at Djedeyde; and when the army returned to Yembo, those that could be mustered did not exceed that number. Scarcity of food also obliged the owners of these remaining horses to sell them, and the men were sent back to Cairo that they might be fresh mounted. As soon as

Tousoun's failure was known to his father, every effort was made to supply the loss and prepare for a new expedition. Mohammed Aly sent large sums of money to his son for distribution among the neighbouring Bedouin sheikhs, with the hope of detaching them from the Wahaby interests. The whole spring and summer of 1812 were spent in these endeavours, while daily reinforcements of troops and ammunition arrived at Yembo. Mahrouky succeeded at last, by the influence of gold, to gain over a considerable number of the Beni Harb, and principally the strong branches of that tribe called Beni Sálem and Beni Sobh, who occupied the pass of Szafra and Djedeyde. Even Sherif Ghaleb, when he was convinced that Mohammed Aly had resolved to prolong the contest, resumed his old system of policy, and assured Tousoun Bey, that he had only joined the Wahabys at Beder from fear, renewed his offer of opening the gates of Djidda and Mekka to the Turkish troops, as soon as the latter should have taken Medinah.

In October, 1812, Tousoun thought himself sufficiently strong to make a second attempt upon Medinah. The Bedouins on the road had become his friends; many individuals of the Djeheyne tribe had enlisted under his banners; and information that the Wahabys remained inactive in Nedjd, encouraged his hopes of success. He transferred his own head-quarters to Beder, and Ahmed Bonaparte took the command of the troops; who, by the same pass which had been the scene of their former defeat, now advanced towards Medinah. They passed unmolested, left a strong garrison at Djedeyde, and arrived without a skirmish before the walls of Medinah.

A Wahaby garrison had occupied that town and its castle since the last year; and both were well stocked with provisions for a long siege. The chief, however, had remained in Hedjaz unaccountably inactive; but the victory at Djedeyde had extended his authority over all the Northern Arabs; and in 1812, he collected tribute from the Bedouins immediately near to Baghdad, Aleppo, and Damascus. Having sold at Mekka the plunder obtained at Djedeyde, he had returned to Derayeh; and his soldiers were so elated by their victory, and so much despised the Turks for their cowardly conduct at Djedeyde, that they considered it in their power, at any time, to defeat them again. Saoud probably expected that Medinah would make a long resistance, and that want of provisions would force the Turks at last to retreat; in which case he foresaw that the Beni Harb would abandon their foreign allies, who, in their turn, might be easily annihilated.

Some skirmishes with the Wahaby garrison took place before Medinah, in consequence of which, Ahmed Bonaparte entered the suburbs, and drove the Wahabys into the inner town; from whence, on the approach of the Turks, they had expelled all the inhabitants, who now resided in the suburbs, and took an active part in the first skirmish against the Wahaby intruders. The inner town was defended by a strong and high wall, and a fortified castle; to batter which the Turks had nothing but light field-pieces. After a siege of fourteen or fifteen days, during which the Wahabys made several sorties, the Turks laid a mine, but in so open a manner, that the Wahabys found means to countermine it, and destroy the work. A second mine was attended with greater success, in the middle of November, 1812; and while the Wahabys were engaged in their mid-day prayers, part of the wall was blown up, and the Arnauts rushed into the town. The Wahabys surprised, fled towards the castle: about one thousand of them were butchered in the streets; the whole town was plundered, and only fifty Turks were killed. The Scotchman above mentioned, Thomas Keith (or Ibrahim Aga), evinced his usual intrepidity on this occasion, being the first who entered the breach. About fifteen hundred Wahabys sought refuge in the castle, which the Turks were unable to take, not having proper battering artillery; and the building, situated on a solid rock, was proof against any mine. But after three weeks, their provisions being exhausted, the Wahabys capitulated, on the promise of Ahmed Bonaparte to grant them safe-conduct: he also agreed that they should carry off unmolested all their baggage; and that camels should be provided for those who wished to return to Nedjd.

When the garrison marched out from the castle, they found but fifty camels, instead of three hundred, that had been promised for their conveyance. Thus, they were obliged to leave behind the greatest part of their baggage, carrying on their own backs whatever was most valuable; but they had no sooner left the precincts of the town, than the Turkish soldiers pursued, stripped, and killed as many of them as they could reach; and few escaped, besides those who were mounted on camels. These Arabs were mostly of the Asyr tribe, residing southward of Mekka, who afterwards made such obstinate resistance against Mohammed Aly. One of their chiefs, Saleh Ibn Saleh, a man from Baghdad, was fortunate in returning to his own country. Masaoud el Medheyan, whom Saoud had made chief of all the Beni Harb, and had placed over several other tribes, not wishing to shut himself in the interior of the town, retired with his family, and forty of his men, to a garden-house, which he had fortified, in a date grove about an hour's distance from Medinah. When this town was taken, he capitulated, on condition of safe-conduct for himself, his family, his followers, and all their baggage; and a house was assigned for his accommodation in the suburbs, where he deposited his family and goods. But when the castle surrendered, and the garrison was so basely massacred, the Turks plundered his house, killed his sons and his attendants, and put himself in irons, and sent him to Yembo. On his passage through Beder, he contrived to escape at night into the mountains, and took refuge with some Bedouins of Beni Harb, who, after three days, were induced by Turkish gold to deliver him up. He was then sent from Yembo to Cairo, and afterwards to Constantinople, where his head was cut off. His fellow sufferer, on this occasion, was Hassan el Kaladjy, already mentioned, who had usurped the government of Medinah, before the Wahabys took the town.

The treacherous behaviour of the Turks at Medinah was an unwise measure, as they were contending with an enemy celebrated for the most scrupulous observance of good faith, in executing the promises of safe-conduct once given. It disgusted all the Bedouins; and with other transactions of a similar nature, which I shall hereafter notice, branded the name of Turk with infamy throughout Hedjaz. Ahmed Bonaparte, in the true style of a Vandal, collected the skulls of all the Wahabys killed at Medinah, and constructed with them a kind of tower, on the high road to Yembo. He stationed a guard near it: notwithstanding which, the Arabs, and even the people of Medinah, succeeded in removing, from time to time, most of those ghastly memorials; and when I arrived at Medinah in 1815, very few of them remained.

On the taking of Medinah, an expedition of one thousand horse, and five hundred foot-soldiers, who had gone by Yembo, advanced towards Djidda and Mekka. They were commanded by Mustafa Bey, the brother-in-law of Mohammed Aly. Like Ahmed Bonaparte, this man had formerly distinguished himself by his barbarous severity towards Egyptian rebels, against whom Mohammed

Aly had such frequent occasion to contend. He was named governor of the province of Sherkieh, where he exterminated whole camps of Bedouins, and burnt many villages; and he was often heard to boast, that more men had died under the sticks of his *kowas* (or executioners), than could have come into the world, had some one of his women produced a male infant every day in the year.

Sherif Ghaleb had been intimidated by the fall of Medinah: perhaps he actually wished to shake off the Wahabys, and for the present, at least, preferred the Osmanlys. He sent messengers to Mustafa Bey, inviting him to his towns. A few hundred men were detached to Djidda, while the principal corps advanced towards Mekka, where El Medhayfe was then commander of the Wahaby forces; but he found himself not sufficiently strong to offer battle, and retired towards Tayf, a few hours before Mustafa Bey made his entry, in January, 1813. The property of the Mekkans was respected, as it had formerly been by the Wahabys; and Ghaleb now joined the Turks with above one thousand Arabs and black slaves. A fortnight after the deliverance of Mekka, an attack was made on Tayf (three days distant eastward), and some skirmishing occurred before the town; El Medhayfe fled; and Sherif Ghaleb, with Mustafa Bey, entered the place, which the Wahabys had held during ten years, and which had suffered more than any other town in Hedjaz.

Mohammed Aly Pasha proceeds from Egypt with an army of Turks—Arrives at Djidda and Mekka—Arrests Sherif Ghâleb, and sends him prisoner to Cairo—Ghâleb's troops assemble at Taraba.

MUSTAFA BEY, intoxicated with success, and with the raisin wine of Tayf, considered himself alone able to subdue the Wahabys. The town of Taraba, distant from Tayf about seventy or eighty miles, in an easterly direction, was one of the principal strong-holds that connected the Wahabys of Nedjd with those of the Yemen mountains. At Taraba resided the Begoum Arabs; and since the Wahaby wars with Sherif Ghaleb, they had fortified their town with a wall and a ditch; and the thick forest of date-trees in which it was situated, served as an additional defence. Mustafa Bey pushed on towards Taraba, but was opposed in the mountainous country, and obliged to return, with a loss of four or five hundred men, to Tayf. Othman el Medhayfe, with his light cavalry, was not inactive in the mean while: he scoured the country in every direction, cut off many stragglers, often intercepted the communication with Mekka, and, during the whole summer of 1812, greatly embarrassed the garrison of Tayf. Sherif Ghaleb, who had, like Othman, his Bedouin horsemen, offered five thousand dollars as a reward for the capture of Medhayfe. Personal enmity to his brother-in-law, who had been the main cause of all his misfortunes with the Wahabys, here overcame his judgment; and he did not reflect, that if the Bedouins about Mekka should lose that chief, the Turks would find it easy to establish themselves firmly in the country, and to deprive himself of his authority.

In one of his excursions Medhayfe halted at Byssel, a small castle which he had built in the mountains, four or five hours eastward of Tayf. The Sherif, informed of his being there, detached a strong party of troops from Tayf, who surrounded the castle and soon after set it on fire. Medhayfe with about thirty followers, all dressed like Bedouins of the poorest class, rushed upon the enemy and cut their way through them; a wound, however, disabled his mare, and she could not carry him far. He then proceeded on foot and escaped from his pursuers; but next day, seeking refuge in the tent of an Ateybe Bedouin, he was seized and carried before the Sherif, who paid the promised reward to the Bedouin and loaded his prisoner with chains. Medhayfe was then despatched to Djidda and Cairo, and finally to Constantinople, where the youngest son of Mohammed Aly presented the noble captive to his sovereign, with the keys of the holy cities and many valuable offerings. As may be supposed, Medhayfe was, soon after his arrival, beheaded; and thus the Wahabys lost their most active and daring partisan in Hedjaz. He was made prisoner in September 1812.

Hedjaz was now reduced to obedience, and the holy cities were free. The pilgrim-caravan from Cairo arrived at Mekka in

November 1812, with all its usual pomp, and performed the hadj with due ceremony. The caravan from Syria could not as yet attempt to pass through the Desert, as the castles in the hadj route and the reservoirs attached to them had not been repaired, nor had stores been provided. Ahmed Bonaparte had returned to Cairo; Tousoun Bey, created Pasha of Djidda, had come to Mekka as a hadjy in the winter of 1812, leaving the Diwan Effendi, an officer of Mohammed Aly's court, as governor at Medinah.

Although the five cities of Hedjaz were now in the hands of the Turks, yet the Wahaby power was unbroken. All the tribes eastward of those mountains that traverse that country from north to east parallel with the sea, still acknowledged the supremacy of Saoud. The Turks, whenever they encountered the Bedouins in the open country, were always defeated; and the Sherif's conduct by no means inspired his allies with confidence. Under these circumstances, Mohammed Aly Pasha thought it necessary to visit in person the scene of action, and strike a signal blow that might establish his authority on a permanent footing in Hedjaz, and enable him to claim for himself the whole merit of the conquest. It was known that his sovereign had peremptorily commanded him to place himself at the head of the troops in that country; and as Egypt, since 1811, was under complete subjection, he had not any excuse for disobedience. The feeble remnant of the Mammelouks had been expelled from Upper Egypt, and had retired to Dongola. Ahmed Aga Lás, a celebrated Arnaut chief, governor of Genne, the only person of influence among the soldiers, and of whose designs the Pasha entertained suspicions, was enticed to Cairo; and his execution was a farther proof (if any were requisite) of the little respect in which Mohammed Aly held his own most solemn pledges of safe-conduct. At his departure from Cairo, Mohammed Aly left Hosseyn Bey as governor of the city and of Lower Egypt, and Ibrahím Pasha, his eldest son, as governor of Upper Egypt, both men of considerable talents; Hosseyn Bey in the military, and Ibrahím Pasha in the civil administration.

Mohammed Aly embarked at Suez with two thousand infantry, while a corps of cavalry equal in numbers, accompanied by a train of eight thousand camels, proceeded by land about the same time. Tousoun Pasha was employed in collecting his troops at Mekka, when his father arrived at Djidda in September 1813. Sherif Ghâleb happened to be there, and repaired on board the Pasha's vessel to compliment him even before his landing. It was on this occasion that they swore upon the Korán, never to attempt any thing contrary to the interest, safety, or life, one of the other—a vow which they solemnly and publicly renewed some weeks after in the holy temple at Mekka, by express desire of the Sherif, who had not yet learned that no promise could be devised sufficiently sacred to bind an Osmanly. The Sherif likewise settled with the Pasha some difficulties which had arisen between him and the Turkish governor of Djidda; for since the conquest of Hedjaz in the sixteenth century by the Turks, it was an established law that the customs of Djidda should be divided between the pasha of that place and the governor of Mekka. Gháleb had appropriated them to his own use exclusively, and the Pasha had promised not to interfere with his possession of them.

Mohammed Aly having arrived at Mekka, bestowed presents on the olemas, and distributed alms to the poor. He began to repair the great temple, and invested large sums for the service, as well as for the ornaments of it. But his first, and most urgent business at that time, was to provide for the transport of necessary supplies from Djidda to Mekka and to Tayf. Djidda had become the great depository of provisions and ammunition for the army. The whole shipping of that port, and of Yembo, (which is considerable,) was employed in that transport business; and Mohammed Aly had contracted with the Imam of Mascat for the hire of twenty ships during one year.

The Pasha had wished that a small frigate, the only ship of war belonging to him, and which was at Alexandria, should have been taken round by the Cape of Good Hope, into the Red Sea; but the English government would not grant permission, knowing that the ship, badly manned as it was, would probably be lost in seas unknown to Turkish navigators, and the loss attributed by the suspicious Turks, to the secret orders of the English. An Englishman, who had resided for some time in Egypt, proposed to convey the ship, at high water, to Cairo, and then upon rollers across the Desert to Suéz. He seemed confident the undertaking was practicable; but his project deviated too much from the usual routine of things to be adopted by the Turks.

It was found more difficult to convey provisions the short distance between Djidda and Mekka, than to send them from Egypt to Djidda. Most of the camels that attended the expeditions to Hedjaz, perished soon after their arrival. By the continual passage of caravans, the herbage in the road was soon consumed, and the camels had no food, except a small quantity of beans in the evening; and of this scanty allowance, some was purloined by the drivers, Egyptian peasants, who had been forced from their homes, and sold the beans to the Hedjaz Bedouins. Of the eight thousand camels which Mohammed

Aly had sent by land, five hundred only remained alive three months after their arrival. To inspect the details of his commissariat, was beneath the dignity of Mohammed Aly; nor could he have made any salutary arrangements without changing the whole administration of his army, in which every individual, from the lowest to the highest, was engaged in peculation. The Bedouins who espoused the Turkish interest were poor in camels, as are all those who live in mountainous districts: few of them ventured to offer their beasts for the service of the army; and during the whole Turkish war there was not, at any time, the number of five hundred Hedjaz camels collected. Under these circumstances, the Pasha found himself crippled in his operations. The actual number of camels could scarcely supply the daily wants of the troops at Mekka and Tayf; and the Pasha offered so little money to the Bedouins, that few of them would employ their camels in his service.

On his arrival, however, at Mekka, finding the necessity of the case urgent, he pressed the Sherif to use all his influence with the neighbouring Arabs, and induce them to furnish as many camels as possible; and for this purpose a large sum of money was advanced, to be distributed among the sheikhs. But a Bedouin chief has no despotic power in his tribe, nor can he forcibly take away the camel of his meanest Arab. The Sherif promised fairly; so did the Arab sheikhs. A second advance of money was demanded from the Pasha, but still no camels appeared.

The Pasha, who during his first residence at Mekka had visited the Sherif on friendly terms, now became cool in his demonstrations of amity. The Sherif, on his side, complained that the customs of Djidda, notwithstanding the promises of Mohammed Aly, were withheld from his officers; and each party soon accused the other of planning insidious machinations. The intimate connexion of the Sherif with all the neighbouring tribes, who, since the capture of Medhayfe, looked upon him as their protector against both Wahabys and Osmanlys, excited additional suspicion in the Pasha's mind; and he became persuaded, that as long as the Sherif retained his authority, he himself could have no chance of pursuing his operations with success. Mohammed Aly had received a firmán from the Sultan, allowing him to act towards the Sherif as he should think expedient; and either to leave him at the head of the government, or to depose and take him prisoner. So, at least, the Pasha publicly declared, after the imprisonment of Sherif Ghálleb.

It now became his principal object to arrest and imprison the Sherif; but this was a difficult undertaking. Ghaleb had with him at Mekka about fifteen hundred fighting men, and other troops at Tayf, and at Djidda. The neighbouring Arabs were all more inclined to favour Ghaleb than the Pasha, against whom it would have been easy to excite their hostility. At Mekka, the Sherif inhabited a strongly-built palace, on the slope of a hill, upon which was a castle, that communicated with the palace by a subterraneous passage. The castle had been built by his elder brother, Serour, and newly fortified by himself, when he heard of Mohammed Aly's preparations for invading

Arabia. The castle was well supplied with provisions; the water was abundant in its cisterns; and a garrison of eight hundred men, with a dozen of heavy guns, constantly defended it. The whole town was commanded by this castle, which might be deemed impregnable with respect to the means which Mohammed Aly could employ towards the capture of it by a regular siege. Many other of Ghaleb's troops, such as sherifs of Mekka, with their attendants, several armed slaves, and mercenary soldiers from Yemen, remained quartered in the town itself, or acted as his body-guards. He soon became aware that Mohammed Aly entertained some treacherous designs against him.

It is certain, that if he had violated his solemn promise, and attacked the Pasha (who had, at that time, but twelve hundred men at Mekka), he might, with the assistance of the Bedouins, have driven him from the town. But whatever accusations may have been made against the Sherif for despotism, his bitterest enemies could never prove him guilty of having broken a promise;

although the Turks insinuate, that he had laid a plan against the person of Mohammed Aly.

Ghaleb no longer visited the Pasha on a familiar footing as before. Whenever he went to see him at his residence (a large school-house, near the great mosque), he was accompanied by several hundred soldiers; and at last, he discontinued his visits altogether, never quitting his palace but on Fridays, when he went to prayers in the mosque. Mohammed Aly in vain attempted to throw him off his guard. He visited him twice, attended only by a few officers, thinking that Ghaleb would return this visit in a similar manner: he had even resolved to seize him in the very mosque, but was dissuaded from so strong a measure by the kadhy, recently arrived from Constantinople, who strenuously maintained the inviolability of that sacred asylum. This circumstance I state on the best authority.

Nearly a fortnight elapsed, during which Mohammed Aly made daily efforts, but in vain, to accomplish his design. At last he devised a stratagem, which proves the great experience he had acquired in the art of entrapping. He directed his son, Tousoun Pasha, who was then at Djidda, to come at a late hour, on a certain evening, to Mekka. Etiquette rendered it necessary that the Sherif should go to salute him; for the omission of such a ceremony would, according to the Turkish notions, have been equivalent to a declaration of war. Ghaleb wishing to pay his visit before any new plans could be devised against him, went at an early hour on the morning after Tousoun's arrival, and called at his house, attended only by a small party. This had been foreseen; and on the day before his son's arrival, Mohammed Aly ordered about a hundred soldiers to conceal themselves in different rooms, adjoining the court-yard of the house where Tousoun was to halt; this they did in such a manner as not to excite any public observation. When Ghaleb arrived, the attendants conducted him up stairs, under pretence that Tousoun was fatigued by his journey; and the Sherif's principal officers were directed to stay below. He entered the Pasha's room and conversed with him for some time, but, when preparing to depart, was informed by *Abdín Bey* (a commander of the Arnauts) that he must remain their prisoner; resistance would have been unavailing; the hidden soldiers rushed from their lurking-places, and Abdín Bey, with Tousoun Pasha, obliged the Sherif to show himself at a window, and order his people below to return home, as no harm was intended.

When this was publicly known, the two sons of Ghaleb took refuge with their troops in the castle and prepared for defence. The Sherif manifested great coolness —" Had I proved a traitor myself, this would not have happened," said he to Tousoun Pasha, in presence of his officers; and when a firman (whether true or forged has not been ascertained) was exhibited, requiring his appearance at Constantinople, he replied, " God's will be done: I have spent my whole life in wars with the Sultan's enemies, and cannot therefore be afraid to appear before him." As long as the castle remained in the hands of Ghaleb's sons, the business was but half done. The Sherif was accordingly forced to write a note to his sons, ordering them to surrender the castle to Mohammed Aly; but he did not sign this order until he was threatened with the loss of his head.

Next day the Turks entered the castle, and the garrison dispersed themselves among the neighbouring Bedouins or went to join the Wahabys. The kadhy, with an officer of the Pasha, and another belonging to the Sherif, were appointed to make an inventory of the whole property of the Sherif, and for this purpose his different palaces at Mekka were closely searched. The amount of all that they found was estimated at about sixteen purses, or two hundred and fifty thousand pounds sterling.

After a few days' captivity at Mekka, the Sherif was sent (in November) to Djidda, where he was detained on board a ship in the harbour, and then embarked for Cosseir. I happened to be at Genne, in Upper Egypt, when he arrived there from Cosseir on the first of January 1814, and had an opportunity of seeing him. His spirits seemed unbroken, he spoke boldly and with great dignity, but never mentioned the name either of Mohammed Aly or of his son. He had with him a dozen of eunuchs, a few Arab servants and two of his sons, who had voluntarily joined him at Djidda. Among the few articles of his baggage, I remarked a handsome chess-board, and it was said that he passed some hours every day in playing chess with his favourite eunuch.

At Cairo he met his women, who had been sent by way of Suez, together with his whole property as it was found in his palaces at Mekka; for Mohammed Aly had received orders not to withhold any part of it. One of his sons died at Alexandria; the other followed his father to Salonika, which the Porte had assigned for his residence, and where he received a monthly pension corresponding to his rank. Some female slaves, a younger son, and a sister of Ghaleb remained at Mekka. The Sherif himself and all his family died of the plague at Salonika in the summer of 1816. Abdallah Ibn Serour, a cousin of Sherif Ghaleb, was seized at Mekka the day after that chief's imprisonment, and forwarded likewise to Cairo. He succeeded in escaping, but was retaken and brought back by the Bedouins of Suez. As he had always been at enmity with Ghaleb, no motive could be assigned for his seizure, but that he had a strong party at Mekka. By orders of the Porte he was soon after liberated.

Sherif Ghaleb, during his government of Mekka, had evinced considerable bravery in fighting against the Wahabys, as well as against his own relations, who often opposed him. His profound cunning, and his intimate knowledge of the Bedouins and their politics, his eloquence and penetration, eminently qualified him for the government of Mekka; but he was rapacious and unjust in making demands of money and levying great fines for the smallest offences, and his avarice had caused him to be generally disliked. During a reign of eight-and-twenty years, he must have accumulated considerable treasures in Mekka, where he lived at little expense. As nothing was found on his removal besides the property above mentioned, many persons suspected that he had privately remitted considerable sums of money or articles of value to the East Indies, particularly to Bombay, with which port he was long engaged in commercial intercourse. Mohammed Aly insinuated that the Sherif had intended to take refuge at Bombay; the care however with which he fortified and stored his castle at Mekka, rather proved that he was determined to resist and even to fight the Turks within the precincts of that holy city.

The capture of Sherif Ghaleb spread terror among all the Mekkans and Bedouins. Several chiefs of the latter, whom he had introduced to Mohammed Aly, and with whom a negotiation had commenced, fled from Mekka, and returned to Taraba, the watering-place of the Wahabys. All Ghaleb's friends at Mekka, and several powerful Sherif families with their adherents, left the city and took refuge in the tents of their neighbours, not knowing whether the Pasha did not design to extirpate the whole Sherif race. Among these was *Sherif Rádjeh*, a distant relation of Ghaleb, and a man the most conspicuous in Hedjaz for courage, judgment, and liberality. To him Mohammed Aly had given the command of a few hundred Bedouins, and had charged him to procure others as recruits in his service. On the day when Ghaleb was seized, Rádjeh left Mekka, and proceeded with all his people to Derayeh, the residence of Saoud, who was glad to be joined by a man of such influence and talent; gave him a considerable sum of money, and appointed him in the room of Medhayfe, to be *Emír el Omera*, or chief of the chiefs of the Hedjaz Bedouins.

The imprisonment of Ghaleb caused a stagnation in all the political affairs of the country. Such open treachery alienated from the Turks even those who were most strongly opposed to the Wahabys, and Mohammed Aly's situation became critical. The best-informed persons thought, that if he had resolved to seize upon the Sherif, he should have waited until some powerful Bedouin sheikhs had joined him, and engaged them to commit actual hostilities against the Wahabys, which might have rendered it difficult or impossible for them afterwards to abandon the Pasha's cause. Mohammed Aly, no doubt, judged of the Sherif's intentions by his own; and feared that he should himself fall a victim to treachery, were he to allow Ghaleb time for the execution of his designs.

But in this he was wrong. Ghaleb was certainly no friend of the Osmanlys; but, on the other hand, he equally disliked the domination of the Wahabys. His project was to weaken both parties; but he never thought of personal treachery towards the Pasha, to preserve whose safety he had made a solemn vow.

A man of the Sherif race, Yahya, distantly related to Ghaleb, and formerly his antagonist, was appointed governor of Mekka by Mohammed Aly, who knew him to be without talents or reputation, and meant that he should be nothing more than a cipher. The Pasha took into his own hands all Sherif Ghaleb's income at Djidda and Mekka, allowing to Yahya a monthly stipend of thirty purses; so that he became, in fact, little more than one of Mohammed Aly's own officers.

At this time, Mohammed Aly had no other object than to forward provisions from Djidda to Mekka and Tayf. Having collected a small quantity at the latter place, he resolved to strike a decisive blow against his enemies, who had been emboldened by his long inactivity, to carry off camels from the very gates of Tayf and of Mekka, while the Bedouins began to show contempt for the power of the Pasha, whom they already detested for his treachery. Among the enemies of the Turks near Mekka, none had evinced more determined hostility than the Begoum Arabs, who inhabited Taraba, and, on a former occasion, had defeated Mustafa Bey. Most of Ghaleb's troops had taken refuge in Taraba after the capture of their master; and Sherif Rádjeh had fixed his head-quarters there, and was joined by Aly el Medhayfe (brother of Othman above mentioned), a man of influence in this country. So that Taraba became the point of union for all the southern Wahabys, as Derayeh was of the northern.

The Begoum Arabs headed by a woman, regarded as a sorceress by the Turks, who are defeated at Taraba—Mohammed Aly takes Gonfode—Discontent of the Turkish troops—Death of Saoud—His son Abdallah declared chief of the Wahabys.

THE Begoum Arabs, of whom some are shepherds, and some cultivators, were headed by a widow named *Ghálye*, whose husband had been one of the chief men at Taraba. She herself possessed more wealth than any Arab family in the neighbourhood. She distributed money and provisions among all the poor of her tribe, who were ready to fight the Turks. Her table was open to all faithful Wahabys, whose chiefs held their councils in her house; and as the old lady was celebrated for sound judgment, and an accurate knowledge of the interests of the surrounding tribes, her voice was not only heard in council, but generally prevailed; and she actually governed the Begoums, although they had a nominal chief, or sheikh, called *Ibn Khorshán*. From the first defeat of Mustafa Bey, near Taraba, the name of Ghálye had spread over the whole country. The Turkish soldiers' fears soon magnified her influence and importance: they regarded her as chief of the united Wahabys, and reported the most absurd stories respecting her powers as a sorceress, bestowing her personal favours on all the Wahaby leaders, who, by her means, were rendered invincible.

These reports served to discourage the Osmanlys, and inspired the Bedouins with additional confidence; thus contributing very materially to cause the failure of Tousoun Pasha's expedition. Mohammed Aly had finally determined to try a second attack; and Tousoun was despatched from Tayf about the end of October, or beginning of November, 1813, with two thousand men, to take possession of Taraba. The country between that town and Tayf was in the hands of hostile tribes, the Beni Sad, El Nasera, and particularly the Ateybe. These had appeared neutral while the Sherif governed; and several of their sheikhs had even come to Mekka, that they might negotiate with the Pasha; but as soon as he seized the Sherif, they all fled back to their mountains, and began to make incursions against Tayf, and the Turkish troops, whom they upbraided with the Pasha's treachery.

When Tousoun marched from Tayf, he took with him provisions for thirty days, of which time he consumed the greater part in a fatiguing warfare against the Ateybes, whom he hunted about in their mountains, reducing some of their branch tribes to subjection. On his arrival before Taraba, he had but three days' allowance of provisions remaining. The troops were immediately ordered to attack the place; but the Arabs defended their walls with spirit, being animated by the presence and exhortations of Ghalye; while the Turks, having no prospect of a rich booty, and fatigued by previous exertions, were easily repulsed. Tousoun commanded a second attack to be made on the next day, but his troops openly refused to contend with Ghalye; and his officers represented the exhausted condition of the army, and the want of provisions, stating, that in case of a second repulse, they should all perish from famine. They thus induced him to change the order for attack into one for a retreat towards Tayf. The Bedouins, aware of his embarrassing situation, as soon as he began to retreat, issued from the town, pressed closely upon his soldiers, gained the passes through which his road lay, and harassed them so severely, that at last the Turks commenced a running fight, and abandoned their baggage, tents, guns, and provisions.

Here Thomas Keith, the Scotchman above celebrated, distinguished himself; with a few of his horsemen he retook a gun, and pointed it so well, that he gave the fugitives time to cross a defile, where otherwise they would probably have been all destroyed. Upwards of seven hundred men were killed in this retreat; many died from mere want of water and provisions; for even before Taraba, a pound of biscuit had risen to the price of a dollar. The army was saved from annihilation by about a hundred horsemen, who accompanied Tousoun. The Bedouin infantry were unable to withstand the charge of this heavy Egyptian cavalry, which, however, had but few opportunities of acting with effect in these hilly and rocky districts. The nimble and hardy sons of the Desert possessed great advantages over the clumsy Turkish foot soldier, who is not capable of enduring much fatigue.

After four days of considerable hardship, and many hair-breadth scapes, Tousoun Pasha arrived with the remains of his army from Taraba at Tayf. The failure of his expedition may be chiefly ascribed to the want of camels, for the transport of his men, as well as provisions. Nor were any spare camels left at Tayf, to furnish him with fresh supplies of both. With no other advantage than experience derived from misfortunes, Mohammed Aly was obliged, after this signal defeat, to resume his former occupation, of sending caravans backwards and forwards between Djidda, Mekka, and Tayf, being convinced that any operations against his enemies could best be directed from the last-mentioned place.

The Wahabys having pursued the Turks within a day's journey from Tayf, returned to Taraba, and again practised their system of harassing, by flying excursions, the Pasha's caravans; which could never effect their passage through the country without such numerous guards, as consumed one-third of the food before their arrival at the place of destination. Mohammed Aly passed his time at Mekka and at Djidda.

In November 1813, the pilgrimage was performed with great pomp. Soleyman, Pasha of Damascus, had come with the Syrian caravan through the Desert without any obstacle; but the Bedouins, through whose territories his road lay, obliged him to pay the passage tribute for the whole space of ten years, during which there had been a suspension of the Syrian hadj to Hedjaz. Great numbers of pilgrims from Asia Minor and Constantinople had come by Suez and Djidda to Mekka, and the inhabitants of the holy cities rejoiced to see the revival of those profits which they had formerly derived from the presence of the pilgrims, and of which they had been partly deprived by the Wahabys. Several thousand camels were sent from Cairo with the hadj caravan to the Pasha, also a considerable reinforcement of troops, while Mustafa Bey was ordered back to Egypt, that he might thence procure fresh horses in place of the vast numbers that he had lost. During the winter of 1813 and the beginning of 1814, the Turkish army remained perfectly inactive.

Every expedition against the enemy having failed, (except that in which Medinah was taken,) the Pasha thought it necessary to attempt a diversion on a new plan, the success of which might encourage his troops, and draw off the attention of the Wahabys from the main point of attack. A naval expedition was fitted out at Djidda, accompanied by fifteen hundred foot-soldiers, and numerous transports loaded with provisions. Hosseyn Aga and Saym Oglu were entrusted with the command of this force. They proceeded to Gonfode, a sea-port, seven days southward of Djidda, and formerly part of

Sherif Ghâleb's territory, but during the last five years in the possession of Támy, sheikh of the Asyr Arabs, the strongest of the mountain tribes south of Mekka, and the most enthusiastic adherents of the Wahabys. The position of Gonfode seemed advantageous in directing attacks against the mountaineers in concert with the garrison of Tayf; and as the place might be easily supplied with provisions, and was a step towards the conquest of Yemen, the riches of which no doubt had strongly attracted Mohammed Aly, the plan was altogether not injudiciously contrived. Gonfode, where Tamy kept only a small garrison, was taken in March 1814, without bloodshed; but most of the inhabitants had fled. A corps of four hundred cavalry set out for Djidda on the sea-shore, as soon as the capture of the town became known. Gonfode was sufficiently defended by a wall to resist an enemy who wanted guns, like the Wahabys; but it has no water within its precincts, and the wells which supply it are three hours distant near the mountains. Fortifications should have been constructed about these wells, and the road from them to the town of Gonfode protected by a line of towers or batteries, as the Turks had abundance of artillery with them; but similar precautions never occur to the stupid and improvident mind of an Osmanly chief: thus the wells of Djidda, which are at half an hour's distance from that town, were always left without the slightest defence.

One hundred and fifty Arnauts were placed near the wells of Gonfode; not so much to guard them against the enemy as to prevent the neighbouring Arabs and country people from watering their cattle. After the Turks had remained at Gonfode about one month, perfectly inactive, they were surprised early in May by a corps of from eight to ten thousand Wahabys, under the personal command of Támy. The Arnauts near the wells were first attacked. Some of them fought bravely till night, the others fled towards the town and spread a general consternation. Without attempting resistance from within the walls, the panic-struck commander and most of his troops ran towards the ships that lay in the harbour, while the Wahabys entered the town and killed numbers of soldiers and servants belonging to the Turkish army, who could not save themselves in boats and who were not able to swim. Many were actually slain in the water close to the vessels, by the Wahabys who swam after them; and the Turkish commander was no sooner safe on board ship himself, than he ordered the sails to be hoisted, and abandoned to certain death all who could not escape by sea.

The Wahabys had never found such booty as rewarded them at Gonfode. The whole baggage, considerable stores, and all the guns became their property, few of the Turks carrying away more than the clothes which they wore. But the most valuable part of the plunder was four hundred horses and a considerable number of camels.

The ships being badly supplied with water or provisions, many of the Turkish soldiers and sailors died on the passage to Djidda. Yet it was insinuated that the commander, Saym Oglu, regularly washed his hands with fresh water, while his unfortunate attendants were expiring from thirst. He was, however, on the arrival of the expedition at Djidda, appointed governor of the place. The few soldiers who had fought during the day at Gonfode, contrived to escape by night, and twelve of them reached Mekka, where they were rewarded by Mohammed Aly, and allowed to enter another corps, as they had resolved never to serve again under the command of Saym Oglu.

About the time of the expedition to Gonfode, Mohammed Aly had gone to Tayf on account of its healthy climate, and that he might be nearer to the scene of action and to the residence of the Bedouins, with whom he again wished to establish an amicable intercourse. In June 1814, a body of fifteen hundred soldiers, the best infantry of Egypt, arrived from Cairo under Hassan Pasha, a celebrated Arnaut chief, and a faithful adherent of Mohammed Aly, whose fortunes he had shared even before he became Pasha of Egypt. Hassan and his brother Abdín Bey, above mentioned, had reduced Upper Egypt to subjection, and had afterwards co-operated with Mohammed Aly in the massacre of the Mammelouks at Cairo, which was perpetrated wholly by Arnaut soldiers. He had lately shown his zeal, during a short revolution that occurred while the Pasha was absent from Cairo. In December 1813, (or the following January,) Latíf Pasha had excited some suspicion. This man, once a Mammelouk of Mohammed Aly, had been sent with Ismayl Pasha to present the keys of Mekka and Medinah to the Grand Sultán, by whom he was created a pasha of two tails, in compliment to his patron Mohammed Aly. A report became current at Cairo that Mohammed was dead, and the conduct of Latíf Pasha gave reason to suspect that he intended to seize upon the government. It was publicly rumoured that he had received from the Porte a firmán, authorising him to do so whenever an opportunity should offer. The deputy-governor, with Hassan Pasha, immediately adopted measures to check this revolution; and for three days they besieged the palace of Latíf Pasha, who was soon after taken in the dress of a peasant, and beheaded; thus they restored tranquillity.

On his arrival in Hedjaz, Hassan Pasha was sent by Mohammed Aly to establish his head-quarters at Kolach, a small village eight or nine hours eastward of Tayf, on the road to Taraba, situated in a plain beyond the great chain of mountains. Numerous wells rendered this Kolach an important position; and it was in some degree fortified. Tousoun Pasha, who had incurred his father's displeasure, by his inconsiderate attack on Taraba, remained stationed at Mekka.

It was about this time that I myself arrived at Djidda from Sowakin. The state of Turkish affairs in Hedjaz did not by any means promise a favourable issue of the contest. Discontent, and a kind of panic, were universal among the soldiers. The repeated victories gained by the enemy, and the certain death that awaited all Turkish prisoners, rendered the very name of Wahaby a terror among the Pasha's troops. The pay, which in Egypt sufficed for a soldier's comfort, scarcely enabled him in Hedjaz to keep himself from starvation. At Tayf and Medinah the prices of all necessary articles rose to such a height, that the soldier could barely afford to purchase enough of bread and onions as his only food; and three or four months' pay was always in arrear. Even at

Djidda and Mekka, every thing was by two hundred and fifty per cent dearer than in Egypt; so that every man, who had saved a little money before his arrival in Hedjaz, was obliged to expend it in procuring the mere necessaries of life. They were paid, besides, in Egyptian piastres, bad coin, and so much less valuable in Hedjaz than at Cairo, that they lost by this money one-third of their pay. Many sold their fire-arms and clothes, and all, in general, suffered much distress; to relieve which, Mohammed Aly never troubled himself. Many soldiers, camel-drivers, servants, and artists, forfeited their pay, and embarked at Djidda and Yembo for Cairo; but the Pasha soon forbade such a proceeding, under severe penalties. By this prohibition they were much annoyed. A Turkish soldier is at all times a volunteer, and may retire from the service whenever he pleases; but in Hedjaz they found themselves treated as prisoners. Many left their quarters at Tayf and Mekka, and came privately to Djidda, hoping that they might escape on board some vessel. When detected, they were marched back, in chains, to head-quarters; and I myself met once, on the road from Djidda to Mekka, above thirty of them, fastened together by their arms to a long rope; an ignominy which those haughty Osmanlys could never forget.

To these causes of complaint must be added the unwholesome air, and the bad water, which render the low coast of Hedjaz one of the worst climates I know: very few soldiers escaped its influence; and at a moderate calculation, one-fourth of them were unable to do duty. Despondency, arising from illness, without any hope of relief, became general; and Mohammed Aly neglected the only means of encouraging them, and reviving their spirit, which was, to increase their pay, and distribute rewards among the few who had distinguished themselves. But their pay was not increased; and there existed such disorders in the financial department of the army, that every chief was able to curtail his inferiors of some part of their allowance; for which injustice no redress could ever be obtained. From the want of Turkish recruits, numbers of Egyptian Fellahs had been dressed up by the officers, with whom they lived as servants, to fill the ranks.

Mohammed Aly was perhaps the only person of his own court and army who, under these circumstances, did not despair of ultimate success; knowing that his downfall and expulsion from Egypt must be certain, if he should not gain some signal advantage in Arabia. Since his arrival at Tayf, he had endeavoured to re-open a friendly intercourse with the Bedouins; and in this respect partially succeeded, by means of money and patience. In August, 1814, the tribes of Hodeyl, Thekyf, Beni Sad, and part of the Ateybe, entered into a new alliance with him; the three first residing between Mekka and Tayf, and the Ateybe farther eastward. Their sheikhs had come to head-quarters, and about five hundred of their Arabs had enlisted under the banners of Mohammed Aly, who allowed to them nearly double as much pay as his own soldiers received. During my stay at Tayf, in August 1814, when I frequently was at head-quarters, Bedouin chiefs daily arrived, and were sure of being presented with a suit of clothes. The great sheikhs received money whenever they came. Many of them took the money, returned to their tents, and informed the Wahabys of all they had seen at Tayf; others remained neutral; and the Pasha, for the sake of gaining over a few, thought it right to give good words and presents to all. He listened to the discourses, and often deceitful assurances of the Bedouins, with a degree of patience, and seeming good-humour, unusual in an Osmanly of any rank.

Those sons of the Desert addressed him in the most blunt and unceremonious manner, calling him merely by his name, Mohammed Aly. One day an Ateybe Bedouin presented himself before the Pasha, kissed his beard, and exclaimed—"I have abandoned the religion of the Moslims" (or 'True Believers,' as the Wahabys style themselves); "I have adopted the religion of the heretics," (so the Wahabys entitle all those Mohammedans who are not of their own creed); "I have adopted the religion of Mohammed Aly." This unintended blunder caused a general laugh; and the Pasha answered through his interpreter (for he but imperfectly understood Arabic), "I hope you will always be a staunch heretic."

But the Pasha and his principal officers continued almost wholly ignorant of the strength, the interests, and private history of the surrounding tribes, and had no local knowledge of their territories; so that the Bedouins could not place much confidence in any measures of their new ally. Still the Pasha's party daily acquired influence The profusion with which he scattered dollars around him, was felt in the heart of the Wahaby host; and although I doubt whether any Bedouin was ever sincerely attached to his cause, yet numbers affected to be so; and at least abstained from hostility, that they might partake of his bounty Even Sherif Rádjeh, who had taken the lead among his enemies, and had personally distinguished himself on the Wahaby side, during the attack of Tousoun Pasha on Taraba, now made proposals of returning to Mohammed Aly, having reason to be discontented with his brother chiefs.

Hitherto the Pasha's conduct showed that Sherif Ghaleb was the only individual personally disliked by him among the chieftains of Hedjaz, and Rádjeh could clearly prove, that he merely abandoned the Pasha's cause, from the fear of sharing Ghaleb's fate. In September he came to Tayf, and Mohammed Aly received him most graciously, and again placed him at the head of his Bedouin soldiers.

Besides the condescending policy adopted in his intercourse with the Bedouins, Mohammed Aly had done all in his power to conciliate the inhabitants of Hedjaz. Many small duties levied by the Sherif were abolished; the customs at Djidda upon various articles, particularly coffee, were diminished; great sums distributed among the needy and poor of all descriptions, besides quantities of corn. The learned men, and those who held offices about the mosques and schools, received donations; the holy places at Mekka were repaired, and, during his residence there, the Pasha observed most scrupulously the minute and tedious rites prescribed to those who visit the Kaaba, which at Cairo would have afforded him subject for derision; indeed, at Cairo he never took any pains to conceal his sceptical or rather atheistical principles. The Turkish soldiers throughout Hedjaz were ordered to abstain from any insulting language towards the natives; and even severely punished, whenever they indulged in those tyrannical acts so frequently practised in Egypt. No soldier could venture to take things by force, or at half-price, from the market; for, on complaint to the Pasha, or his officers, the natives were always the favoured party. Thus, the strong prejudice of the Arabs against all foreigners became gradually weaker, and the Pasha obtained credit for justice and charity; qualities to which, in Egypt, he could not have made the slightest pretension.

In May 1814 Saoud died of a fever, a disease very prevalent in Nedjd. By this the Wahabys lost an indefatigable leader, possessing all the necessary talents for the eminent situation which he held. It is said that his last words were addressed to his son Abdallah, advising him, "never to engage the Turks in open plains"—a principle which, if strictly followed, would undoubtedly have insured to his people the recovery of Hedjaz. Abdallah, his eldest son, to whom the principal Wahaby chiefs had already paid obeisance during Saoud's life-time, became heir to the supreme authority. Some dispute, however, arose. Saoud had several brothers, who claimed part of his treasures, and one of these brothers, Abdallah, was supported by a strong party of the olemas of Derayeh. But after some short hostilities Abdallah, the son of Saoud, was acknowledged the Wahaby chief. With respect to courage and skill in war, his reputation exceeded that of his father; but he knew not so well as Saoud how to manage the political interests of the tribes under his command, the great sheikhs of which began to assume airs of independence. This impaired the general strength. The southern Wahabys, who were now most exposed to attacks, did not find support from the northern tribes, whose cavalry might have materially assisted them; and even the southern sheikhs were at variance with each other, and the Pasha had to contend against single tribes, rather than a combined force. This want of union, perhaps, may be ascribed to the contempt in which the Turkish troops were held by their enemies.

Distribution of the Turkish forces in Hedjaz — Massacre at Bahra — Mohammed Aly sends his son Tousoun Pasha to Medinah — The Turks defeated by the Wahabys in Zohrán — Mohammed Aly marches from Mekka towards Byssel — The Wahabys defeated there.

IN September 1814 the Pasha's forces were distributed as follows:—About two hundred men were with Ibrahím Aga, the Moherdar, or seal-bearer of Mohammed Aly, at Mekka, where also were one hundred and fifty Arabian soldiers, under Sherif Yahya. Between three and four hundred men, commanded by Diván Effendi, were at Medinah; one hundred formed the garrison of Yembo, and two hundred were stationed at Djidda. Tousoun Pasha, with three hundred and fifty men, was encamped between

Yembo and Medinah. Mohammed Aly had with himself at Tayf three hundred Turks, of whom about one hundred were cavalry. Hassan Pasha commanded the position of Kolach with one thousand of his Arnauts; and his brother, Abdín Bey, commanded the advanced posts of the army, consisting of twelve hundred Arnauts and four hundred cavalry, who had just arrived from Cairo. These advanced posts had pushed forwards three or four days' journies southward of Tayf, into the territory of the Beni Naszera tribe, and towards the district of Zohrán, where sheikh *Bakhroudj*, chief of the Ghamed Arabs, was principal opponent of the Turks. They had the advantage of being quartered in a fertile country, furnishing a sufficiency of corn and barley for their wants: thus they became independent of the magazines at Tayf.

The forces above enumerated may appear very inconsiderable to the reader; yet I am confident that they are here rather overrated than underrated. According to the reports of the Turks, even of the Pasha himself, twenty thousand men were actually under the command of Mohammed Aly The numerous stragglers attending a Turkish army; the multitude of Turkish merchants and hadjys scattered over Hedjaz, who affected the dress of soldiers, from whom they could scarcely be distinguished; an immense train of camel-drivers, grooms, and other servants accompanying the army—all contributed to swell its apparent numbers; and the Wahabys themselves had probably never a clear idea of the real strength of their enemies. Daily reinforcements arrived from Egypt, but were scarcely sufficient to recruit the ranks which had been so much weakened by disease, and by unsuccessful encounters with the Wahabys. The number of troops which Mohammed Aly had in Egypt was too small to admit of many draughts for Hedjaz. While the total amount of troops in this country was five thousand men, those in Egypt never exceeded from six to seven thousand effective soldiers; nor could the Pasha lessen that number without exposing the country to attacks, which he apprehended at once from Constantinople, from the Mammelouks in Dongola, or from England: at that time especially from the last-mentioned quarter.

When it became known in those countries which furnish the greater proportion of soldiers to the Turkish Pashas, namely Albania, Romelia, and the coast of Asia Minor, that the campaign in Hedjaz was so extremely distressing to the troops engaged in it, very few recruits came over to Egypt; and ever since 1813, Mohammed Aly was obliged to keep in those countries his own recruiting officers, who could not accomplish their object without expending considerable sums. I heard the Pasha himself state at Tayf, that his army consisted of 35,000 men; 20,000 of whom were in Hedjaz, and 15,000 in Egypt; and this statement was generally regarded as correct.

To defend the holy cities, and overawe the neighbouring provinces, the small force of between four and five thousand men was quite sufficient, with the help of four hundred Bedouin soldiers, collected from different tribes, and whose pay was twice as much as that allowed to the Turks; but with this army, the Wahabys could not be conquered. Yet it seems that the Pasha, at his departure from Cairo, had solemnly promised to his sovereign, that he should bring them under subjection. Notwithstanding all the Pasha's efforts, the want of camels had not been supplied; the road from Tayf to Mekka, and thence to Djidda, literally strewed with the carcasses of dead camels, showed that a continual renewal of the baggage-train was absolutely necessary. In the suburb of Mekka, called Moabede, where the caravans from Djidda and Tayf halted, so pestilential a stench was produced by the hundreds of dead camels, that on application made by the inhabitants, numerous poor negro pilgrims were hired to fetch dry grass from the adjoining mountains: a quantity of this was piled over each dead camel, and set on fire; so that the carcasses were consumed to ashes. At a moderate calculation, from the beginning of the war in 1811, up to this period, thirty thousand camels belonging to the army had perished in Hedjaz. But few remained in Egypt. Large supplies had been sought in the Negro countries as far as Sennar; but the transport of provisions from

Genne to Cosseir, and from Cairo to Suez, required such numbers that few, comparatively, could be spared for the Hedjaz service. The Pasha had sent an officer to Damascus, that he might purchase camels among the Syrian Bedouins. These camels were expected at Mekka with the next pilgrim caravan; and Ibrahim Pasha had done all in his power to collect among the Libyan tribes as many as could be procured; which were likewise to be sent with the Egyptian hadj to Hedjaz.

Until the time of their arrival, mere defensive measures were adopted. About five hundred camels had been hired from the Harb Arabs for carrying provisions from Djidda to Tayf; but their owners positively refused to advance a step farther towards the east or the south, lest their camels should be taken by the Wahabys. The garrison at Tayf, as I learned there from good authority, had only provisions for ten days; and their distress was so great some weeks after, that the corn brought by caravans was immediately distributed, and never put into store-houses. On the advanced-posts at Kolach, and in Zohran, the troops had no means of grinding the corn; but every soldier received a daily portion of grain, which he was himself obliged to pound between stones, and to bake in the ashes.

Meanwhile the Wahabys made frequent incursions towards Tayf, and against the tribes which had espoused the cause of the Pasha; who, on his side, harassed the enemy's country, by means of his cavalry, sent in small detachments. Sherif Yahya, with his Arabs, made (in August 1814) an expedition over the mountains towards Gonfode, and brought back a valuable booty in camels and sheep. He had no sooner returned to Mekka, than Tamy avenged himself, by sending a corps of six hundred camel-riders of the Kahtan tribe towards Djidda. I myself narrowly escaped from these partisans. Having had occasion to go from Mekka to Djidda with a small caravan of camels, we arrived about midnight at a watering-place called Bahra, half way between the two towns, where a small camp of horsemen was stationed to guard the road. These men we found in a state of alarm, some Bedouins from the south having just informed them, that the enemy was approaching. Our caravan immediately went off towards the northern mountains, and by a circuitous route arrived at Djidda the next day; but we had scarcely left Bahra, when the Wahabys rushed into it. We heard the discharges of musketry, and were soon after informed, that the invaders massacred all the inhabitants whom they could find, pillaged the camp and baggage, and carried away a small caravan, which had halted at Bahra some time before our arrival. All this time the eighty horsemen never offered the least resistance, but galloped off towards Mekka, where they spread the greatest consternation.

The intercourse between Djidda and Mekka was thus interrupted during a whole week; but the Wahabys, having accomplished their purpose, retreated to their homes. They had set out from a distance of at least fifteen days' journeys to plunder on this road; and their exact knowledge of the country enabled them to take such a route as brought them suddenly on their prey. In this kind of warfare the Bedouins have always been distinguished; and their invariable success in such enterprises terrified the Turkish soldiers more than the loss of a regular battle could have done; because they never thought themselves secure for one moment, as soon as they had left the precincts of the towns.

Ever since the taking of Medinah, the Turkish troops had remained there completely inactive, as the supplies sent to them from Yembo were scarcely sufficient for their daily use, and for the inhabitants of the town. The tribe of Harb continued on amicable terms with the Turks; and their sheikh, *Djezye*, who had mainly assisted in taking the place, had gone, in June 1814, on business to the Divan Effendi, commanding there. Being one day seated in full council with the latter, and unable to endure the vain Turk's idle bragging, he exclaimed in hearing of the whole company—" Be silent, O Divan Effendi, as every body knows that it was I who paved the way for your entrance into this town; and were it not for this blade (here he clapped his hand upon his sword), no Turk would have ever entered

Medinah."[1] The Turkish commander was incensed at this address, insulted Djezye with the most opprobrious terms, struck him, and caused him to be put in chains; and next day it was reported, that he had killed himself in prison, certain proofs having been obtained that he was carrying on a treasonable correspondence with the Wahabys. The consequence of such an event might have easily been foretold. As soon as the Beni Harb knew that their sheikh was killed, they shut the road through their mountains against the caravans from Yembo; and without actually joining the Wahabys, they committed partial hostilities upon the Turkish out-posts.

In hopes of settling these disturbances, Mohammed Aly ordered his son, Tousoun Pasha, (in August 1814) to proceed towards Medinah. He arrived in September at Beder, and found that the Harb Arabs had strongly garrisoned the pass of Djedeyde, and were resolved to oppose his entrance by force. They boldly demanded the life of the Divan Effendi, as an expiation of the murder of their sheikh. Fortunately the Divan Effendi died at that very time, not without strong suspicion of poison, and the Arabs became more inclined to a reconciliation. Their new sheikh and minor chiefs received valuable presents; the price of Djezye's blood was paid to his relations, in compliance with the Bedouin custom, and peace was again concluded with the Beni Harb. Having passed the defile, Tousoun Pasha arrived at Medinah in October 1814, with about three hundred foot-soldiers and five hundred horse; most of the latter had just come from Cairo. The horsemen took up a position two or three days' journies in advance of Medinah, at Hanakye, whence they made several excursions towards the territories of the northern Wahaby tribes.

About this time, the affairs of the Turks assumed a favourable aspect throughout Hedjaz; and hopes were entertained, that after the reinforcement of men and camels, expected with the hadj, should arrive, the Pasha might be enabled to conduct in person some grand enterprise against the enemy; when another defeat still farther humbled the pride of the Turks, which, notwithstanding their cowardice, and their failures in war, they had never relinquished. Abdín Bey, with his Arnauts, occupied, as I have said, some districts in the province of Zohran, south of Tayf. To prevent the daily attacks of his enemies, he had laid waste the country within forty miles, and totally destroyed whatever might be serviceable for the passage of troops. He was encamped on one side of this artificial desert, and Bakhroudj was posted on another (the southern) side of it. With the usual negligence of Turkish commanders, no intrenchments were thrown up, no advanced posts nor sentinels placed towards the enemy; whose general was thus enabled, at the head of his own, and several allied tribes, and a strong detachment of infantry from Tamy, to surprise the Turks. Bakhroudj, early one morning in September, fell upon the sleeping Arnauts, who scarcely waited to fire one shot, but abandoned their camp, and all that it contained. Some little resistance was made by a few hundred soldiers from Romelia, under Mahou Beg, the Pasha's most active chief in Hedjaz; but they could not long contend against the overwhelming force of the Wahabys; and the whole army owed its escape from destruction to a corps of cavalry commanded by a Syrian chief, named Hosseyn Bey, who covered their retreat, in which Bakhroudj pursued them during two days. The Turks once more lost all their tents, artillery, baggage, and provisions: eight hundred Turkish foot-soldiers, and eighty horsemen, were killed; and it was not until the remainder of the army arrived at Lye (about four hours from Tayf) that they ventured to take up a position. Here Abdín Bey received some reinforcements from Tayf and Kolach; and as it was known that the Arabs had returned home, he advanced a second time, by the Pasha's orders, towards Zohran. But such a panic had seized the Turkish troops, that one half of them deserted, and came to Tayf; and Abdín Bey was obliged to fix his head-quarters at a short distance in advance of Lye, wanting the necessary complement of men.

This last defeat had a very depressing effect on the spirits of the troops. Abdín Bey had hitherto enjoyed the highest reputation for skill and courage, and his troops were certainly the best of the whole army; but the late disasters convinced his soldiers, already not much inclined to fighting, that further resistance against such numerous enemies as the Wahabys would be vain, and there was not a man among the Turks who did not long to find himself again safe in Egypt. As the Turks however understand better almost than any other nation "faire bonne mine à mauvais jeu," they described their last defeat as a victory, because the horsemen had brought the heads of about sixty Wahabys with them to Tayf; and while the army trembled within the walls of that town, guns were fired at Djidda to announce a victory; Cairo, also, was illuminated three days, to celebrate the glorious exploit of Abdín Bey.

Soon after this event, a very seasonable reinforcement of cavalry arrived from Cairo. Horsemen had been drawn from all the Libyan tribes of Bedouins who encamp during summer in the neighbourhood of the Nile valley, and eight hundred of them had been despatched to Hedjaz. These were themselves Bedouins, well accustomed to the system of warfare prevalent among the Wahabys, their horses were equally trained to fatigue as the riders, and every horseman had a camel with him, carrying provisions for the most distant expedition. Half of these horsemen had joined Tousoun Pasha on his way to Medinah, the others advanced to Tayf, and had no sooner arrived there, than they distinguished themselves by daring excursions against the Wahaby tribes, situated several days' journies eastward of Taraba, being accompanied by Bedouin guides of those countries. They were all armed with guns and pistols, and known as good marksmen; circumstances which rendered them very formidable to their enemies. In one of their excursions they brought away eight thousand sheep from a Wahaby encampment.

The pilgrim-caravans arrived in November from Syria and Egypt. With the former came three thousand camels, which Mohammed Aly had purchased from the Syrian Bedouins, Tousoun Pasha having taken at Medinah, from the caravans passing, one thousand of the original number, four thousand to relieve his own want of transport-camels, as much felt at Medinah as in the southern parts of Hedjaz. The Egyptian caravan likewise brought about two thousand five hundred camels, besides a reinforcement of one thousand Turkish horsemen. And that these might be all employed for military purposes, the whole caravan was detained at Mekka, and the mahmal sent, after the pilgrimage was over, by sea back to Suez. This caravan, I must here remark, was entirely composed of soldiers or public officers; all the private pilgrims having been ordered to proceed by sea.

The Pasha came down from Tayf to assist in the ceremony of the hadj, and to meet Soleyman, Pasha of Damascus, who had again accompanied the caravan from Syria. Mohammed Aly's favourite lady, the mother of Tousoun, had come by sea to perform the pilgrimage. Her retinue was as splendid as the wealth of Egypt could render it. Four hundred camels transported her baggage from Djidda to Mekka, and her tent, pitched at the foot of Mount Arafat, equalled in size and magnificence any thing of which we read in fairy tales or Arabian romances.

Several personages of high rank had come from Constantinople to visit the Kaaba; and the pilgrimage of this year, at which I myself assisted, was performed by about eighty thousand persons of all descriptions and nations. After the ceremony, the Syrian caravan generally remains a few days at Mekka. Mohammed Aly, however, on this occasion protracted their stay ten days beyond the usual term, by requiring all their camels (amounting to above twelve thousand) for the purpose of carrying provisions between Djidda and Mekka to supply his troops.

When he had collected his whole effective strength between Mekka and Tayf, and the state of his storehouses and the number of his camps excited his hopes of success against the enemy, he declared his intention of placing himself at the head of the army, which served to raise in some degree the spirits of his troops. Taraba was again pointed out as the first object of attack. A well-appointed artillery, consisting of twelve field-pieces, encouraged the soldiers to believe that the walls of Taraba could not long remain standing, and that no man should be required to scale the wall, as had been the case when Tousoun Pasha made his attack. Five hundred axes were provided for cutting down the palm-trees which impeded the approach to Taraba. Twenty masons and as many carpenters were attached to the army for the purpose of opening a mine which was to blow up the enemy at once. That the soldiers might be rendered sure of success, a load of water-melon seeds was brought from Wady Fatme and carried in pomp through the town of Mekka, it being intended, after the total demolition of Taraba, to sow these seeds on the spot where it had stood. But these preparations, so far from tranquillising the minds of the soldiers, increased their uneasiness, as they proved what vast importance was attached to the taking of that place, and the difficulty of the enterprise.

The enemy laughed when it was reported that Mohammed Aly considered the taking of Taraba as certain; and about this time the Pasha received a letter from Sheikh Bakhroudj, written in that sneering and taunting style, of which Arabian history affords many examples. He told him, that he had already sufficient proofs of what the Wahabys could do; that if he resolved to fight with them, he ought to provide better troops than those which he now commanded; but that his wisest plan would be, to return again into Egypt, and indulge in the sweet water of the Nile. Bakhroudj, as will hereafter appear, atoned, by an ignominious death, for this affront to the dignity of a Turkish Pasha.

As an encouragement to the army, thirteen Bedouins of the Ateybe tribe, captured on the Djidda road, and accused of being Wahaby robbers, (although it afterwards appeared most clearly, that they had gone to Djidda for the purchasing of provisions,) were executed on a plain near Mekka, before an immense multitude of people. One man of the same party, at the moment when his hands were untied, and a Turkish soldier prepared to inflict the deadly blow, knocked him down, and escaped through the crowd. He might ultimately have saved his life, had he sought refuge in the mountains, instead of continuing to run along the plain, where he was overtaken, and cut down, by a Turkish hadjy, who happened to be there on horseback. On this occasion the lower classes of the natives evinced their strong dislike of the Turks; they loudly hissed, and cursed the soldiers, who cruelly mangled their unfortunate victims: the fugitive was encouraged in his attempt to escape by shouts of applause; while the hadjy who killed him was abused in most opprobrious terms, and loaded with execrations.

Every thing being now prepared for the expedition, which was to decide the fate of this campaign, Ahmed Bonaparte left Mekka with the greater part of the infantry on the 15th of December, 1815, and proceeded at once to Kolach. The Pasha intended to follow him with about twelve hundred cavalry, on the 24th; when intelligence arrived, that a strong Wahaby force had been seen in the neighbourhood of Gonfode, advancing towards Djidda. This report excited great alarm. Bedouin scouts were despatched to obtain information; and at Djidda considerable disorder prevailed, for it was expected that the Wahabys, if they should not attack the town itself, would cut off its communication with Mekka. For some time water had been extremely scarce at Djidda; the government cisterns were now hastily filled by compulsory measures; and the inhabitants drew their scanty supply from wells at a distance of three hours. Every kind of provisions in Mekka rose thirty per cent. on the first rumour; but the people recovered from their panic, when it was known that a small troop only of Tamy's soldiers had pitched their tents near Gonfode.

A few days after, news arrived that Bakh roudj had made an incursion into the territories of the Naszera Arabs, allies of the Pasha, and had completely sacked the fortified village of *Bedjíle*, their principal hold, where a garrison of Arnauts had been stationed. It was once the head-quarters of Abdín Bey. News likewise arrived, mentioning that Taraba was in a state of considerable preparation, and that reinforcements were hastening from all quarters towards that town, to defend it against the threatened attack.

On the 26th of Moharram, 1230, (or the 7th of January, 1815,) Mohammed Aly Pasha marched from Mekka with all the troops and camels that he could muster, proceeding towards Kolach, where Hassan Pasha, Abdín Bey, Mahou Bey, Ahmed Bonaparte, Topous Oglou, Sherif Radjeh, and other chiefs of his army were already assembled, and where sufficient provisions for fifty or sixty days had been collected. When he arrived at Zeyme (which is the second station on the northern road from Mekka to Tayf) and Kolach, express messengers, sent in great haste from the last-mentioned place, informed him that a considerable body of the enemy had seized upon Byssel, between Tayf and Kolach, intercepting the communication between these places, while another hostile corps had made an incursion eastward of Kolach against the Ateybe Bedouins, allies of the Turks. Mohammed Aly hastened his march towards Kolach, where he arrived on Wednesday, and despatching Sherif Rádjeh with his Bedouin soldiers and the Libyan horsemen to support the Ateybe, advanced on Thursday himself with all his cavalry towards Byssel. He found the Wahabys encamped on the side of the mountains which open towards the plains of Kolach. They had possession of several fine watering-places, while the Turkish soldiers carried the water for their own use upon camels, from Kolach. The Wahaby force has been variously estimated; according to the best information, it amounted to about twenty-five thousand men, infantry, and a few cavalry; the mountains here being poor in horses, and the Wahabys when engaged in distant expeditions, seldom employing any considerable number of cavalry, depending chiefly on their camel-riders and matchlock foot-soldiers.

Their army was accompanied by five thousand camels, but wanted artillery of every kind. It consisted of men chosen among the southern Wahabys and a small band of the northern, the latter being themselves kept in check at present by the hostile demonstrations of Tousoun Pasha at Medinah. All the chiefs of the Yemen mountains, and of the south-eastern plain, were with the army, as was Faysal, the son of Saoud, and brother of the present Wahaby chief. Among the former, Tamy, sheikh of Asyr, and Ibn Melha, the agyd, or war-chief, of that tribe, held the first rank; and one-third of the army was composed of their Arabs; Ibn Katnan, sheikh of the Sabya Arabs, Ibn Khorshan, chief of Taraba, Ibn Shokban, chief of Beishe, Bakhroudj, sheikh of the Arabs of Ghamed and Zohran, Ibn Dahman, sheikh of the Shomran Arabs, Ibn Katamel, chief to part of Ateybe, who remained attached to the Wahaby interest; Ibn Mahy, a chief of the Dowasir Arabs, who live far to the south-east, towards Hadramaut, and many other equally renowned and powerful leaders, commanded different bodies of this army. In making a diversion against Gonfode, they had endeavoured to draw off the Pasha's attention from the main object of attack, and fell quite unexpectedly upon Byssel, where they occupied a strong position in the very centre of the Turkish lines. When the Pasha's cavalry approached, they remained upon their mountains, and repulsed an attack made on a valley, where Mohammed Aly wished to plant one of his field-pieces. The whole of Thursday was consumed in several fruitless attempts made by the Turkish cavalry, of whom, in their last attack, above twenty were killed by the lances of the Wahaby horsemen.

Although but few lives were sacrificed this day, the Turks began to despair of success, while the Wahabys entertained sanguine hopes of weakening the enemy by repeated defeats, and finally destroying them. Fearing such a result, several Turkish soldiers, as well as Bedouins in the Pasha's service, deserted from the army and hastened back to Mekka, which they reached on the following Saturday night. Here they spread the news of a complete defeat, of the Pasha's death, and other disasters.

The terror caused by these reports in Mekka can scarcely be imagined. I resided there myself at that time, and can speak of it as an eye-witness. Numerous stragglers belonging to the army, and Turkish hadjys preparing to return home; also Turkish merchants and such soldiers as were in the town, all expected to suffer death on the first arrival of the victorious Wahabys. Four hundred piastres were offered for a camel to convey a person to Djidda; but the few Bedouins who possessed camels, removed them into the mountains on the first rumours of defeat. Several people left Mekka on foot that very evening, and endeavoured to reach Djidda by the next morning. Others joined the garrison in the castle, and put on Bedouin rags that they might not be supposed foreigners; but nobody prepared for defence, and Sherif Yahya himself, although he had not received any official report, was ready for a sudden flight to Djidda. For my own part, being convinced that if the Pasha had been defeated, the Wahaby light troops would intercept all fugitives on the Djidda road, and preclude the possibility of escape, I thought my safest asylum would be the great mosque, which, at all times, the Wahabys had respected as an inviolable sanctuary. Having put into a bag the few valuable articles that I possessed, along with a good provision of biscuit, I went accompanied by my slave and established myself in the mosque, where many poor hadjys had from the same motive taken up their residence. My biscuit, with the water of Zemzem found in the mosque, might have supplied my wants for some weeks. That the whole crowd of Turks did not follow this example, may be ascribed to their judging of the Wahabys by themselves; for they could never believe that in the hour of victory a soldier would regard any place as sacred.

But our apprehensions proved to be founded on imaginary disasters; and, after a night of considerable anxiety, we were surprised and gratified the next morning by the official account stating the total defeat of the dreaded Wahabys. Mohammed Aly Pasha had clearly seen, during the skirmishes on Thursday, that he could have no chance of success as long as the enemy remained upon the mountain; he likewise knew, that if unsuccessful on the following day, his career both in Hedjaz and in Egypt would probably close for ever. Therefore he sent, during the night, for reinforcements from Kolach, and ordered two thousand of his infantry, together with the artillery, to take a position in flank of the Wahabys. The next morning at an early hour he renewed the attack with his cavalry, and was again repulsed. He then assembled his officers, and commanded them to advance with their columns closer to the position of the Wahabys than they had done before, and, after firing off the guns, to retreat in seeming disorder. This was accordingly executed. The Wahabys seeing the enemy fly, thought that the fortunate moment for completely crushing them had arrived; they left their strong-hold on the mountain side, and pursued the flying Turks over the plain. All happened as the Pasha had expected. When he thought the enemy sufficiently distant from the mountains, he rallied his cavalry, faced the pursuers, and the battle was soon decided in his favour.

The Turkish infantry now turned the position of the Arabs. Sherif Rádjeh who had just arrived with his corps, after having repulsed the enemy's false attack upon the Ateybe, joined Mohammed Aly, beset the valley through which the Wahabys were to retreat, and thus compelled them to fly in the utmost disorder. For pursuing a vanquished foe, the Turkish soldiers are pre-eminently qualified. As soon as Mohammed Aly saw the enemy running, he proclaimed among his troops, that six dollars should be given for every Wahaby's head. In a few hours five thousand were piled up before him: in one narrow valley fifteen hundred Wahabys had been surrounded and cut to pieces. Their whole camp and baggage, and most of their camels, became a prey to the Turks. Tamy himself escaped with only a few followers.

About three hundred Wahabys were taken alive, at the express command of Mohammed Aly, who ordered his men to offer them quarter, as very few of the enemy had condescended to beg for mercy. Sherif Radjeh was despatched with some cavalry in pursuit of the fugitives, and he was joined by many of the neighbouring Arabs, who would probably have exhibited as much zeal against the Turks, if the Wahabys had been victorious.

In this battle the Pasha fought personally, at the moment when he ordered his cavalry to wheel about and face their pursuers. He deserves great credit for his dispositions during the night previous to that attack, and for having known how to keep up a spirit of resistance in his troops, who had already relinquished all hopes of success. On his side, no man distinguished himself more than Sherif Radjeh; mounted upon a famous mare, and, armed with his lance, he galloped far in advance of the army, and among crowds of the enemy, towards the tent of Faysal, the most conspicuous in the whole camp, and, striking his lance into the ground before it, defended himself with his sword against a number of Wahabys, until his friends approached, and rescued him. When Mohammed Aly soon after passed near this spot, he inquired of Radjeh, to whom that tent belonged. "To Faysal," he replied. "Then take it," said the Pasha, "with all that it contains." Besides the camels, no booty of great value was taken by the army. Radjeh found in the tent of Faysal about two thousand dollars only. Many quarrels occurred between the Turkish soldiers and their allies, the Bedouins, who accompanied Radjeh, repecting the division of plunder. The Pasha seemed inclined to favour the Bedouins; and most of the camels fell to their lot. It was stated, that the Turks lost on this day between four and five hundred men.

The defeat of the Wahabys may be wholly attributed to their having descended from the mountain into the plain, where they had no means of resisting the Turkish cavalry. Saoud, in the last words which he addressed to his son, had cautioned him against such a proceeding. But the contempt in which the Wahabys held the Turkish troops, and the desire of terminating the campaign, and perhaps of securing the person of Mohammed Aly himself, made them forget the wise system of warfare which they had hitherto adopted; and their astonishment on finding themselves so suddenly overpowered, rendered them incapable of resistance.

Some anecdotes, however, are related of signal courage evinced by the Wahabys. Ibn Shokban, with a few hundred men, fought his way through the whole Turkish infantry, and escaped. Bakhroudj, one of the wildest of the Wahaby chiefs, killed with his own hand two of the Pasha's officers; and when his horse was shot under him, mixed among the Turkish cavalry until he found an opportunity of pulling a man from his horse, which he mounted, and by this means escaped.

Whole parties of the Asyr Arabs were found upon the mountains tied with ropes together by the legs. On parting from their families, they had all sworn by the divorce (an oath common among Bedouins, and strictly observed, see Vol. i. p. 277.) not to fly before the Turks, and if possible to return victorious. Being unsuccessful in battle, they resolved, at least, to prevent each other from running away. They fought as long as their ammunition lasted, and were then cut to pieces.

Turks elated with victory—their cruelty—their distresses on the march from Beishe—Mohammed Aly returns to Mekka—Makes proposals of peace to Abdallah Ibn Sàoud.

MESSENGERS were immediately despatched to Constantinople and Cairo with intelligence of the victory; and throughout Hedjaz the Turks became elated, and resumed their national insolence and fierceness, which latterly they had, in some degree laid aside. Meanwhile the natives of Hedjaz, although glad to be secured against a second Wahaby conquest, grieved to see Arabians vanquished by Turks, and shuddered at the cruelties which these victors had practised, both during and after the battle. The three hundred prisoners, to whom quarter had been promised, were sent by Mohammed Aly to

Mekka. In the true style of a Turkish conqueror, he celebrated his triumph by causing fifty of them to be impaled before the gates of Mekka; twelve to suffer a like horrible death at every one of the ten coffeehouses, halting-places between Mekka and Djidda; and the rest before the Mekka gate of Djidda: there they were left until the dogs and vultures devoured their carcasses. If the Turks delighted in this disgusting and atrocious act, which they styled a martial triumph, all the Bedouins, their allies, expressed aloud the utmost indignation; and Sherif Radjeh remonstrated with the Pasha, but in vain.

Four days after the battle Mohammed Aly, with due activity, arrived before Taraba; from which Faysal fled at his approach. The inhabitants, abandoned by their allies, capitulated; and the Pasha fixed his headquarters at that place for some time. The Turks plundered a few houses, and carried off some handsome Arab women, who were, however, restored to their families by the Pasha's order. Ghalye had taken refuge with the Bedouins. She might have been sent as a trophy to Constantinople; but no proposals could induce her to return, or confide in the offers of the Turks. Immediately after the victory at Byssel, the Pasha directed Sherif Yahya to proceed by land with his Arabs to Gonfode; and he reinforced his corps with the troops of Mahou Bey. Orders also were sent to Djidda, that several transports, loaded with provisions, might be despatched to Gonfode. As the strength of his enemies lay in the southern countries, Mohammed Aly resolved to carry the war into their own territories, and completely to exterminate their party. Whatever provisions could be procured at Kolach, were loaded upon the five or six thousand camels, which the army had in its train on leaving Mekka, and upon almost as many which were taken after the battle.

The army proceeded from Taraba through the territory of the *Oklob* Arabs, in a southern direction, towards Rannye, over a level ground, two days distant, occupied by the Sabya Arabs, whose sheikh, Ibn Katnan, had fortified there a small castle, which surrendered. After four days' journies from that place, they arrived in the district of Beishe, a fertile country belonging to the powerful tribe of Beni Salem, whose chief, Ibn Shokban, was a leading man among the Wahaby party. Here two small castles had been built by the express command of Saoud, who had strengthened all the principal positions of these countries by similar structures. Ibn Shokban had taken refuge after the battle in the tents of some neighbouring Bedouins of the Kahtan tribe. One of those castles opened its gate: in the other, Ibn Shaban, a second chief of Beni Salem, defended himself for four days against the whole Turkish infantry, commanded by Hassan Pasha; while Mohammed Aly with his cavalry had taken post in the date-groves, on the southern side of Beishe.

Proposals for a capitulation were offered to Shaban, on condition of safe-conduct; these he unfortunately accepted; and with his garrison, of about sixty men, marched from the castle, and received camels for the carrying of his baggage. But having gone to pay his respects in the tent of Hassan Pasha, this fanatical Turk reproached him with heresy. Shaban boldly defended his opinions, and retorted upon the accuser, who became so enraged that when Shaban and his followers quitted the tent, he ordered his soldiers to fall upon them, and they were all cut to pieces. Of such infamous transactions, which frequently occur, no notice is ever taken by Turkish rulers.

The army remained about a fortnight at Beishe, the most important position in the country eastward of the Yemen mountains, and called by the northern Bedouins the key of Yemen. Here the Pasha was joined by many Bedouins. All those who were discontented with the Wahabys, and all the relations of those sheikhs who had been turned out of their situations, came now to seek redress from Mohammed Aly; who, imitating the system of Saoud, changed every where the chiefs of tribes, by which means a strong party in his favour was created. News reached him here, that Tamy had again assembled a considerable army in his mountains, and had resolved to try the chance of battle a second time. It was towards his territory that Mohammed Aly now directed his march, taking a western course from Beishe.

On this march his army suffered the extremes of hunger and fatigue. Half of the camels had already perished before the arrival of the troops at Beishe, and many horses had shared the same fate. The van-guard cleared the road of every particle of stubble or blade of grass; so that those who came after, found nothing but a barren desert. On the Turks' approach the Arabs fled in all directions, carrying off their cattle and provisions, while the Bedouins themselves who followed the army, took advantage of the general disorder, and purloined many loads. At every halt a number of camels dropped, and their flesh was greedily devoured by the soldiers. The last biscuits had been distributed at Beishe, after which every man was left to supply himself as well as he could. The Pasha found it necessary to allow the troops an additional pay of one piastre per day, but this money was of little use in a place where as much corn made into bread, as would satisfy a man's appetite once, cost twelve piastres.

At two days' journey from Beishe, they entered the mountainous country, which had been almost totally deserted by the people. Among the Shomran Arabs, the Turks enjoyed a few days' repose. Hassan el Sulsan, a Bedouin chief, descended from an individual who, three centuries before, when Othman Pasha conquered Yemen, in the reign of Selim the Great, had been placed at the head of this tribe, was now reinstated by Mohammed Aly in the ancient rights of his family. Here in one day a hundred horses died: the soldiers became dissatisfied; but as they clearly saw that a retreat would lead to inevitable destruction, they still advanced. The Pasha commanded all his chiefs to dismount, and to march on foot at the head of their respective columns. To his soldiers he promised a glorious booty, in plundering the towns of Yemen, thus endeavouring to keep up their spirits. A market was established at every halt, just before the Pasha's tent, where the allied Bedouins sold to the troops whatever they had been able to carry off from the Arabs on the road. The Pasha himself presided, and enforced strict order.

Near the territory of Asyr the rugged mountains presented many obstacles to the passage of artillery. This territory the Turkish army entered twelve or fourteen days after they left Beishe, halting near the castle called Tor, which stood upon an elevated ground, surrounded by mountains. It had been built by Abou Nokta, the predecessor of Tamy, and was deemed so strong, that no Arab force could possibly take it. Here Tamy had collected from eight to ten thousand men, whom the Pasha attacked: and as at Byssel, the Turkish troops were repulsed on the first day. The Asyrs fired incessantly, and three hundred Turks were killed. Tamy was seen on horseback in front of his men, animating them by war-songs. The field-pieces having been brought to bear on the second day, the Wahabys gave way. Tamy himself fled, but was the last who quitted the field. The battle was better disputed than that of Byssel, the number of Bedouins who accompanied the Turks rendering them more powerful than their enemies. In the castle were found considerable stores of provisions, which proved most serviceable to the army, likewise ammunition, the guns taken from Gonfode the year before, and a large stock of matchlocks, old Persian barrels, particularly esteemed by the Arabs.

After Radjeh had been sent in pursuit of Tamy, and a new sheikh of the Asyr, called Ibn Medry appointed, Mohammed Aly descended the mountains through steep passes to the sea-shore. It appears that he wished to advance towards Yemen, from the less mountainous country at the western foot of the high chain. Sherif Hamoud (surnamed Abou Mesmár) was in possession of the seacoast. He had formerly been of the Wahaby party, after many contests with them, but when the Turks arrived in Hedjaz, he sent an envoy to the Pasha with rich presents, assuring him of his readiness to support the Turkish interest; the frequent defeats, however, of the Turks, caused his zeal to subside; he opened a communication with Tamy, and an envoy sent to his court by Mohammed Aly, found him engaged in active preparations for war. Little doubt existed that his design was to join the Wahabys if the Turkish expedition should miscarry. The Pasha had long eagerly wished to riot in the far-famed wealth of Yemen, which, however, is probably much overrated in the East. He might also have wished to get possession of the dollars which annually were sent in great sums from Cairo to purchase coffee; and it was reported in Hedjaz, that in case of success against the Wahabys, he had resolved to attack Hamoud. For this reason he had opened a correspondence with the Imam of Sanaa, who had sent presents to him, and was cordially interested in the favourable issue of his enterprise, as it would have delivered him from two dangerous neighbours, the Wahabys and Hamoud.

The army, however, after such a long, fatiguing, and perilous march, showed here strong symptoms of discontent, and openly declared their desire of returning to Mekka; it is certain that, as the means of tranquillising them, Mohammed Aly was obliged to promise that they should soon be sent back to Egypt, and replaced by fresh troops; and instead of proceeding southward, he now directed his march towards Gonfode. Tamy, after the battle which he had lost, took refuge in the neighbourhood of Arysh, at the house of a Sherif, his friend, and a relation of Hamoud. The Sherif thought this a favourable opportunity for warding off a hostile invasion, and of evincing his submission and repentance. Tamy was put in chains, and a messenger despatched to the Turkish headquarters with a letter to Hamoud, in which the Sherif styled himself the "slave of Mohammed Aly," and asked how he should dispose of his prisoner. Sherif Radjeh, who was then roaming about the mountains in search of the fugitive, received orders to take him back to Gonfode, where the army now arrived, and found an abundant supply of provisions brought from Djidda by sea.

Mohammed Aly had sent off a body of troops from Rannye to invade Zohran from the east, while Mahou Bey ascended the mountains from the east, and by a skilful manœuvre placed the Arabs of Bakhroudj between two fires, so that they were defeated, and Bakhroudj himself taken and carried to Gonfode. Here the Pasha remained several days, his two noble captives being lodged in tents close to his own. Tamy's conduct inspired the whole army with respect. The Pasha often conversed with him for amusement, as the tiger plays with his prey before he seizes it in his grasp; but Tamy's dignified behaviour subdued the ferocity even of this Turk, and he promised to write in his favour, and procure him permission from the Sultan to live in retirement in the mountains of Romelia. Tamy was a man of great natural powers; short in stature, with a long white beard, his eyes darting fire; sarcastic in general, but polite towards the Turkish chief. Bakhroudj, on the contrary, observed a sulky silence, convinced that Mohammed Aly would never forgive him for the letter he had once addressed to him, (see p. 307. of this Vol.) nor did the Pasha ever desire to see him. Finding his guards asleep one night, Bakhroudj seized a poniard, contrived to loosen his chains, and escaped from the camp, but was overtaken after he had killed two men and wounded another. Next day Mohammed Aly asked him, "by what right he had killed his soldiers:"—"Whenever I am not chained," replied Bakhroudj, "I act as I please:"—" I shall act in the same manner," said the Pasha ; and to entertain his Turks, and at the sam etime gratify his revenge, he immediately caused the unfortunate prisoner, bound as he was in chains, to be placed in the midst of his body guards, who were directed to wound him slightly with their sabres so that his torments might be prolonged. He at last expired without having uttered one complaint: his head was sent to Cairo and Constantinople along with Tamy, who, upon his arrival in the latter city, was instantly beheaded.*

From Gonfode the Pasha proceeded to Mekka, which he reached on the 21st of March, fifteen days after he had left that city. The nature of his expedition will be comprehended, when I state that out of more than ten thousand camels, originally with the army (half of which were taken at Byssel), only three hundred returned to Mekka; all the rest having perished on

* In violation of the solemn promise made by Mohammed Aly, Tamy, when he arrived at Cairo, was loaded with an immense chain about his neck, placed upon a camel, and then paraded through the streets with the head of Bakhroudj in a bag suspended from his shoulders.

the road. Much of the baggage and ammunition was destroyed, there being no means of transporting it; and of the horses, only three hundred were brought back. Of four thousand Turks who set out from Mekka, only fifteen hundred returned, all of whom were, from the highest in rank to the meanest, worn out with fatigue, and without clothes or money.

Mohammed Aly, according to the promise extorted from him at Gonfode, permitted them all to embark at Djidda, except Hassan Pasha, whom he kept in Hedjaz with a few hundred Arnauts; and soon after, new reinforcements arrived from Egypt.

The strength of the Wahabys was now considerably reduced, particularly in the south. When the battle of Byssel took place, Abdallah Ibn Saoud was with a body of troops in the province of Kasym, ready to oppose the progress of Tousoun Pasha from the side of Medinah; but he returned to Derayeh on learning the defeat of his party, apprehending an attack from Mohammed Aly, who might easily have advanced from Taraba towards Nedjd.

Soon after his arrival at Mekka, the Pasha assembled all the chief men and olemas of the city, and read to them a letter which he had addressed to Abdallah Ibn Saoud, exhorting him to submission and offering terms of peace: he charged him to restore the treasures which his father had taken from the prophet's tomb at Medinah, if he did not wish to share the same fate as his friends in the south. This letter was sent by a Turkish soldier, accompanied by some Bedouins, to Derayeh.

After a short stay at Mekka, Mohammed Aly, having appointed Hassan Pasha governor of that town, left Hosseyn Bey, a cavalry chief, and Sherif Radjeh, in garrison at Taraba and Beishe, and set out for Medinah, where he arrived unexpectedly on the 14th of April, with only thirty or forty attendants, mounted upon dromedaries, having performed the whole journey by land. Tousoun Pasha had already quitted Medinah. Thomas Keith, or Ibrahim Aga, before mentioned, acted meanwhile as governor of that place.

When the news of Mohammed Aly's success became known to the northern tribes, many of their sheikhs made proposals to Tousoun Pasha, who was then at Medinah, offering to join him against the Wahabys, whose power was more severely felt in the north than among the southern tribes. In March, most of the Kasym sheikhs came, one after another, to Medinah, and assured Tousoun Pasha of their readiness to assist him. He bestowed presents on them, and sent back with them four hundred cavalry, to garrison some of their villages. Tousoun himself now conceived hopes of conquering Nedjd. Notwithstanding his great personal courage so often displayed, he had been always unfortunate in his Hedjaz expeditions. He became anxious to emulate his father in the glory he had acquired by his late campaign; but, like most Turks, he did not calculate his means. Mohammed Aly had not entrusted to his son's management any considerable sums of money, knowing his liberality and generous disposition, and perhaps unwilling that any one besides himself should acquire renown in Hedjaz. Tousoun was much in want of camels, and of food, for the neighbouring Bedouins. The prices of all articles were higher at Medinah than at Mekka. Tousoun, however, resolved to try his fortune, and left Medinah at the end of March, setting out for Hanakye, a ruined village with walls, two or three days' journies on the road to Kasym. He had with him about four hundred camels carrying provisions, and between two and three hundred cavalry, with four hundred foot-soldiers. He was followed by a few hundred Bedouins, chiefly belonging to the tribes of Harb and Meteyr.

He remained some time at Hanakye, and was still there when his father arrived at Medinah. The reason of Mohammed Aly's visit to this sacred city was probably his wish to obtain information respecting the affairs of Northern Hedjaz, and pay his devotions at the Prophet's tomb. From Medinah he immediately sent orders, directing Tousoun Pasha to return from Hanakye, that he might concert measures with him for future proceedings. His son, however, had determined on the expedition; and as soon as he received Mohammed Aly's order, instead of obeying it he set out towards Kasym. As he was equal in rank to his father (being like him a pasha of three tails), the latter, perhaps, was wrong in making him feel too strongly his state of dependence; and we must not look for any thing like proper filial sentiments among Turkish grandees. The custom duties of Djidda, which by right belonged to Tousoun, had been transferred by the Porte to Mohammed Aly, for the expenses of the war. Tousoun Pasha received merely a certain allowance by the day, like all the other chiefs of the army; and in placing the north of Hedjaz under his command, Mohammed Aly had associated with him a person of his own court, named Kadery Effendy, through whom all business was to be transacted, and whom Tousoun was advised to consult upon all occasions, as if his father thought him unfit for the high situation that he filled.

Soon after their arrival at Medinah, Kadery Effendy, as might easily be supposed, rendered himself disagreeable to his pupil, who, in a fit of anger, caused him to be beheaded. Great disorder then prevailed in the administration of affairs. The interests of the Turks with the surrounding Arabs were ill managed: the soldiers committed depredations.* Tousoun wanting camels, seized all the cattle that could be found among the Bedouins; and Mohammed Aly, on his arrival, instead of taking offensive measures against the enemy, was fully occupied in repairing the mischief consequent upon the errors of his son. Two hundred and fifty horsemen, under the command of Thomas Keith (or Ibrahim Aga), were despatched after Tousoun Pasha, as was likewise a detachment of infantry, who had arrived from Yembo, having as their chief Ahmed Bonaparte, just returned from Cairo. Tousoun, early in May, after a march of ten or eleven days from Medinah, reached the province of Kasym. During this journey he attacked the Heteym Bedouins, and carried off five hundred of their camels, which he sent to Medinah for the transport of provisions from

* In January 1815 I arrived at Medinah, and was soon confined to my bed by illness; at this time my slave frequently came home weeping and complaining that the Turkish soldiers had taken from him the meat which he had procured for my use and beaten him because he had attempted to resist.

Yembo. Upon his arrival at *Rass*, one of the principal towns or large villages of Kasym, and defended by a wall, he was joined by the cavalry which had preceded him some time; and the sheikhs of different districts in Kasym came to concert measures with him: but the great chief of Kasym, *Hedjeylan*, did not attend him, having always been sincerely attached to Saoud, and even now to the interests of his son, in whose support he assembled the Arabs of his party at the town called Bereydha.

Abdallah Ibn Saoud enters Kasym with an army—Negotiations between him and Tousoun Pasha—Peace concluded—Mohammed Aly returns to Cairo—Despatches his son Ibrahim Pasha with an army to renew the war in Hedjaz.

In the mean while Abdallah Ibn Saoud had not neglected his duty; with an army composed of Bedouins and settlers of Nedjd, he, likewise, entered the province of Kasym, and fixed his head-quarters at Shenana, only five hours distant from Khabara, where Tousoun Pasha had encamped. But here Tousoun found himself in a precarious situation. He heard that his treasurer, Ibrahim Aga (Thomas Keith), had been surrounded on the road, and, notwithstanding a most gallant resistance, had been cut to pieces, together with all his horsemen. The fertile district of Kasym might have supplied provisions for a much larger army than his, but the light troops of the Wahabys were hovering about the Turks, who depended wholly upon two or three villages for their daily food, which they foresaw must soon become extremely scarce. The road to Medinah was occupied by the enemy, and no intelligence could be obtained respecting the steps taken by Mohammed Aly.

Tousoun Pasha could not place much confidence in the Bedouins who were with him, knowing that they would readily join the other party on the first disaster of the Turks. He wished to terminate all suspense by a battle, but his officers and soldiery were not willing. The superior numbers of the Wahabys frightened them; they felt convinced that in case of defeat not one man could escape, and they thought it more prudent to compromise with the enemy than to fight; the more so as Mohammed Aly had empowered his son to make peace, if that could be done on favourable conditions. Some Bedouins were employed to sound the disposition of the enemy's chief, who, when he knew the circumstance, sent Habab, one of his people, to find out what were actually the designs of Tousoun, offering safe-conduct to any one who might be despatched to the Wahaby camp. However favourable these matters seemed to Abdallah, he foresaw that the destruction even of Tousoun's entire force of about twelve hundred men, would be of little real advantage to him. It would oblige Mohammed Aly to direct all his strength against that point, the consequences of which would be of more detriment to the Wahaby cause than the partial victory could be of service to it. He knew besides, that the resources of Egypt were such as would enable Mohammed Aly to prolong the campaign in Hedjaz for any time. The Turks had suffered many defeats, but had always repaired their losses and became stronger after each. They also possessed the means of bribery, and the Wahaby chief well knew that some of his present companions were in their hearts his enemies; by making peace he could insure the dependence of those tribes which had not yet joined the Turkish party.

Habab was well received by Tousoun, who immediately sent Yahya Effendy, his physician, a native of Syria, who spoke Arabic better than any of the Turks, to negotiate with Abdallah. He was the bearer of some presents, and remained three days in the Wahaby camp. As both parties desired peace, the negotiation was soon concluded, and one of Abdallah's courtiers waited upon Tousoun that he might ratify the treaty. In this, Abdallah renounced all claim to the possession of the holy cities—affected to style himself a dutiful subject of the Sultán, and obtained a free passage for all his party through the Turkish dominions, which would enable him to perform the pilgrimage at pleasure. Tousoun Pasha abandoned to Abdallah Ibn Saoud, those towns of Kasym which he held in his possession, and dismissed from his party all the sheikhs of that country who had already joined him. He likewise ceded to him all those Bedouin tribes whose pasture-grounds lay beyond Hanakye, reserving to himself those only which resided between Hanakye and Medinah, and in the territories of the holy cities. Nothing was said of the Southern Wahabys; in consequence of this, immediately after Tousoun went away, Abdallah punished the Bedouins (particularly the Meteyr tribe) who had joined his enemies. As both parties apprehended treachery, some difficulties arose respecting the priority of departure. Abdallah at length consented to break up his camp, but insisted that four of the Pasha's chief officers should be left with him as hostages until his arrival in a safe position, when he was to send them back. Tousoun, probably to conceal his own weakness, cavilled for some time on this point. A correspondence took place, and several of Abdallah's original letters are now in my possession. Most of them exhibit that frankness and boldness of language by which the Bedouins have always been distinguished, widely differing from the ceremonious and complimentary style usual among other eastern nations in similar cases. They were all written under the immediate dictation of Abdallah himself, expressing the unfeigned sentiments which he felt at the moment, and the hand-writing shows that but little time was employed in committing those sentiments to paper.

Tousoun Pasha then returned from Khabara to Rass, and, after a residence of twenty-eight days in the province of Kasym, arrived at Medinah about the end of June, 1815. With him were two Wahabys, envoys from Abdallah to Mohammed Aly, bearing the articles of peace, and a letter from their chief to the Pasha, and another for the Grand Sultán.

Tousoun did not find his father at Medinah; for being convinced that the actual resources and means of war in those northern parts of Hedjaz were not sufficient to authorise hopes of success, Mohammed Aly resolved on leaving the doubtful chance to his son, rather than incur the risk of diminishing the reputation which he had himself acquired. On this occasion he evinced great want of paternal feeling. While Tousoun was absent, not one messenger was ever despatched to him; so that he remained ignorant of all that was passing at Medinah, and other places. Mohammed Aly, besides, thought so little of his son's necessities, that he left him without a single piastre; and when Tousoun arrived at Medinah, he was obliged to borrow money for his daily expenses. There was perhaps a cogent reason why Mohammed Aly quitted Medinah, and finally Hedjaz. In February and March, 1815, apprehensions were entertained in Egypt of an attack to be made upon Alexandria by the Capitan Pasha of the Grand Signor, who had arrived from the sea of Marmora with a strong fleet, and was cruising in the Archipelago. Alexandria and Rosetta were reinforced with numerous troops; and the Kechya Bey, governor of Cairo, sent messengers in haste, by land and sea, to acquaint Mohammed Aly of the circumstance.

On the 19th of May, some weeks after I had quitted Yembo, on my return to Cairo, Selim Aga, governor of Yembo, received an express from Medinah, ordering him, on pain of death, to have a ship ready for sailing on that very evening. Next day Mohammed Aly, with a few of his suite, mounted upon dromedaries, arrived at Yembo, and, without waiting for refreshment on shore, hastened to the ship, and immediately set sail. The Pasha would not allow the captain to keep along the coast, as is usual, although he knew that the ship was but scantily supplied with water, but made him stand out into the open sea, straight for Cosseir.

On his landing at that place, he could not procure either a horse or camel, but mounted, without loss of time, an ass, that he might proceed through the Desert to Genne, and hasten down the Nile. The dread of an attack upon Alexandria had, in the mean time, subsided: this he heard, and therefore travelled more leisurely towards his capital, which he reached on the 25th of June, 1815, after an absence of nearly two years, during which his health had considerably suffered from the climate of Arabia. He did not then know that peace had been concluded with the Wahabys; but that his arrival might be attended with éclat, the taking of Derayeh by Tousoun Pasha was announced, and the complete annihilation of the Wahabys.

In the month of August, after Mohammed Aly's return to Egypt, most of those very troops who had accompanied him in the Arabian campaign, showed symptoms of insurrection. The corps of Mahou Bey, and others, began to pillage the capital; and the Pasha found it necessary to shut himself up in his caste at Cairo. Those troops, to whom fine promises had been made in Hedjaz, now found that regulations were proposed, which would considerably reduce their pay, and increase their fatigues. The Pasha desired to introduce the *Nizâm Jedíd*, or new system of discipline, a measure which had proved fatal to Sultan Selim; but the insurrection stopped its progress; and Mohammed Aly could not venture to punish the revolters. The reputation which he had acquired in Hedjaz was found to have caused a change in his character. The affability that had distinguished him from other Pashas was converted into haughtiness: instead of a simple soldier-like establishment, he began to indulge in pomp and show, and monopolised all the exports and imports for his own advantage, by which the labourers and manufacturers were materially injured.

The two envoys sent by Abdallah Ibn

Saoud, in the train of Tousoun Pasha to Medinah, arrived at Cairo in August, during this insurrection of the soldiers. One of them, named Abd el Azyz, was a relation of the great founder of the Wahaby sect, Abd el Waháb: the other was an officer of Saoud. They presented to Mohammed Aly the treaty made with his son, Tousoun Pasha, and the letters before mentioned. Abd el Azyz was a very learned man; and several of the most able olemas of Cairo were directed by the Pasha to dispute with him on theological subjects. He inquired into every circumstance concerning the civil and military establishments of Egypt, its resources and commerce: he purchased several Arabic books, and at last excited the jealousy of Mohammed Aly, who ordered two or three soldiers to attend the envoys at all times, wherever they went. This conduct rendered their situation so unpleasant, that they soon demanded leave to depart. A suit of clothes, and three hundred dollars, were given to each as presents, with a letter to Abdallah Ibn Saoud from the Pasha, written in a most ambiguous manner, respecting peace or war;

offering to confirm the treaty concluded with his son, provided the Wahabys would cede to him the province of Hassa, one of the most fertile and important of their dominions, being situated on the Persian Gulf.

It now became manifest, either that Tousoun Pasha had deceived the Wahabys at Kasym, or that Mohammed Aly had given a fresh proof of the contempt in which he held all engagements. Tousoun, equal in rank with his father, had concluded a treaty, binding his whole party; and he had enjoyed the full benefit of that treaty, in being allowed to save himself and his army from destruction. His father, however, seemed anxious to represent the matter under a different point of view at Constantinople; and as he had pledged himself to annihilate the Wahabys, by taking Derayeh, it was necessary to persuade his sovereign, that he had not yet abandoned that object; and that the treaty concluded by his son should be merely considered as a temporary armistice.

In September 1815 Sherif Rádjeh, the Arab hero, was brought to Cairo in chains.

It was said, that he had quarrelled with Hassan Pasha, governor of Mekka, who suspected him of a treasonable correspondence with the enemy. But the fact was, that all the Osmanly party regarded him with jealousy, on account of the high renown he had acquired, and the general report, that the victory at Byssel was gained by his exertions. During the first months of his confinement at Cairo, he was treated like a common criminal; but in spring 1816, when preparations were made for an expedition against the Wahabys, he was released from prison, and Mohammed Aly affected to show him marks of distinction. On the 7th of November, 1815, Tousoun Pasha arrived at Cairo with a few hundred soldiers. After his return to Medinah, communication was restored all over Hedjaz with the Wahabys. Caravans came from Nedjd to Medinah and Mekka; and in December, many Wahabys attended the pilgrimage. No Turkish chief had exerted himself so much as Tousoun during this war, or displayed more personal valour; but his efforts had always been unsuccessful. He was welcomed at Cairo with all the honours due to his rank and bravery; but on paying a visit to his father at Alexandria, he was very coldly received.*

About the close of 1815, several Arab sheikhs from Hedjaz came to Cairo, claiming the Pasha's protection. They were relations of Ibn Medry, whom Mohammed Aly had appointed chief of the Asyr Arabs in place of Tamy; but when he returned to Cairo, Tamy's party obliged the new sheikhs to fly, Hassan Pasha being unable to support them Mohammed Aly received them politely at Cairo, gave them some presents and sent them back to Mekka, but could not at that time spare any troops for Hedjaz; being seriously engaged in preparations for defending the Mediterranean coast against an attack, which, according to general report, the English intended. He had already heard, when in Hedjaz, of the first peace of Paris and the fall of Bonaparte, and had become apprehen-

* In September 1816 Tousoun Pasha died of the plague at Rosetta, where he commanded a large body of troops, encamped there for the defence of the coast. He was regretted as a man who showed great attachment to his friends, and was profuse in the expenditure of money.

sive that England would send a large army from the south of France to Egypt, which he fondly supposed was the darling object of all European powers. These apprehensions were renewed by the second treaty of Paris, and still more when the English took possession of the Seven Islands, which he regarded as stepping-stones towards his own territory. He was confirmed in his opinion by the absurd reports of his own emissaries, and the whispers of flattering and servile Franks, or Pseudo-Europeans, who were all determined Anti-Anglicans. After some months the alarm subsided, and he again directed his views towards Hedjaz, intending to despatch a powerful expedition to that country, under his son, Ibrahim Pasha. Circular letters were written, in January 1816, to all the Arab sheikhs of Hedjaz, apprising them of Ibrahim's speedy departure, exhorting them to assist him; and assuring them, that he designed to revisit their territories himself in a short time, and crown his former victories by the taking of Derayeh. In these letters no mention was made of the treaty concluded with Abdallah Ibn Saoud; nor had any answer yet arrived from the latter, respecting Mohammed Aly's demand of the district of El Hassa.

In March 1816 intelligence arrived, that disturbances had broken out towards the south of Mekka. The Turkish cavalry stationed at Beishe, Rannye, and Taraba, had been withdrawn. Some Bedouins in the Pasha's service remained as the garrison of Taraba. The Wahábys seemed daily to gain strength in those quarters; nor does it appear that the southern districts had ever been included in the peace made with Abdallah Ibn Saoud.

In August 1816 Ibrahim Pasha left Cairo for Hedjaz, with orders, it was said, to attack Derayeh, taking the way of Medinah and Kasym. He was accompanied by about two thousand infantry, who went by Cosseir to Yembo, and fifteen hundred Libyan Bedouin horsemen, who proceeded by land: these horsemen he had himself chosen among the most warlike tribes of the Bedouins in Upper Egypt. In his suite were two French officers, one of whom, a chef d'escadre, had been with Bonaparte at Rochefort; but in consequence of orders to quit France, he repaired to Egypt, where Mohammed Aly received him in a very flattering manner, besides several other French emigrants of the year 1815.

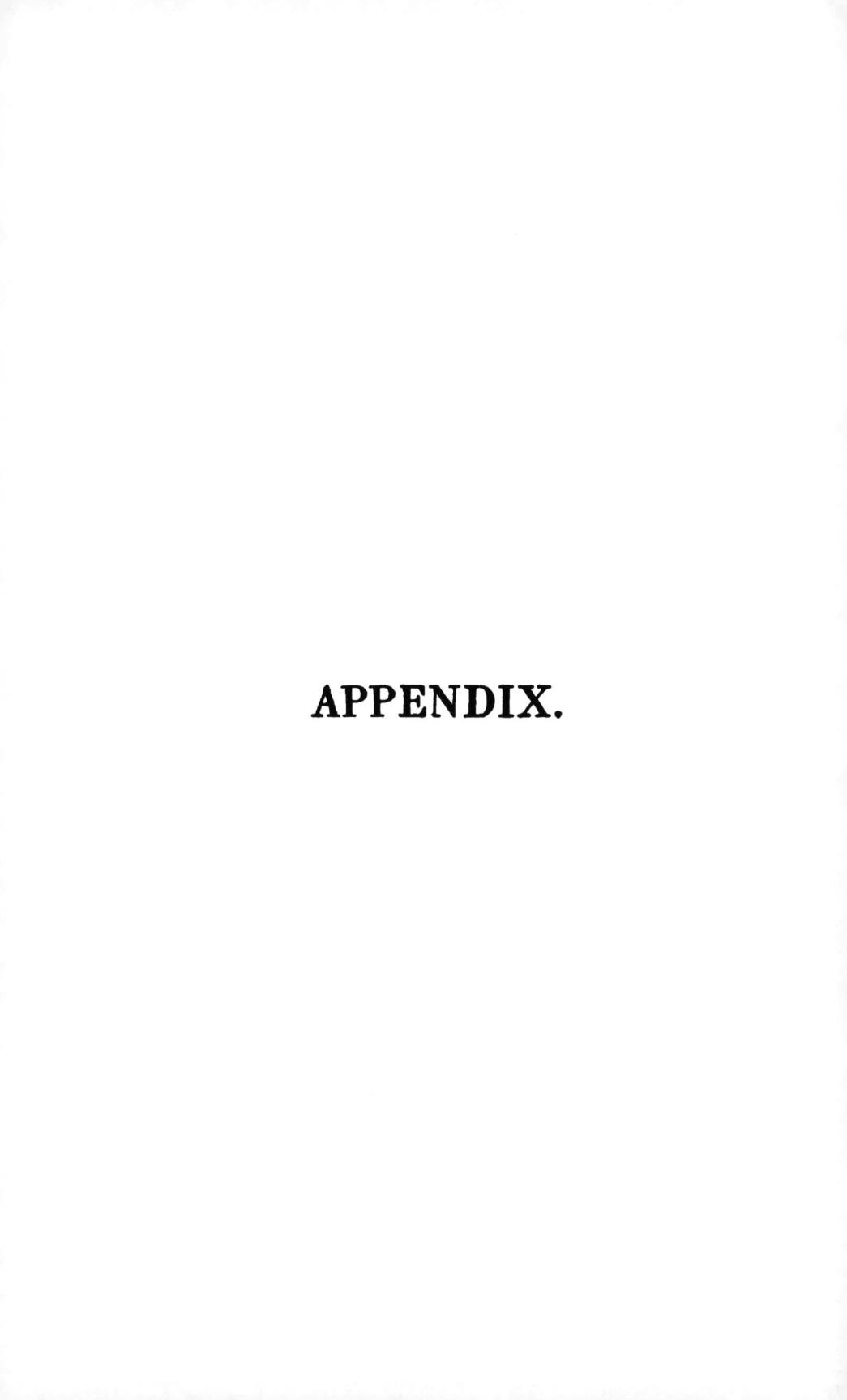

APPENDIX.

APPENDIX.

No. I.

Lunar Months.—(See Vol. I. p. 74.)

The following Table will show the names given by several Bedouin tribes, more particularly the Aenezes, to some of the Mohammedan months.

Moharrem, they call اشور—*Radjeb,* غُرَّة—*Shaban,* قصر. The two months of *Shawál* and *Dsu el Kade,* they call (plurally) الافطار — *Shawál* (singly) فطر الاول; and *Dsu el Kade,* فطر الثاني. The month *Dsu el Hadj,* they call الضحيىر.

No. II.

Warfare of the Bedouins.—(See Vol. I. p. 312.)

While the battle rages, and horsemen or camel-riders contend in single combat, or mix in general fight, flying or pursuing, the Beni Atye (a considerable tribe of Arabs between Syria and the Red Sea, among whose numbers are the Omran, Howeytat, and Terabín) frequently utter with a loud voice the following verses

" You birds with the bald-heads, you Rakham and Hadázy,
" If you desire human flesh, be present on the day of combat."

يا طير يا شايب الراس يا ابو رخم و حدّاذي
ان كان بدكم لحم ناس احضروا يوم الطرادي

The *Rakham* and *Hadázy* are birds of prey—the former an eagle, the latter a falcon. This battle-song is called by the Arabs *Boushán*, بوشان.

No. III.

Blood Revenge.—(See Vol. I. p. 314.)

The origin of the *dye* (ديه), or fine for the blood of a man slain, amounting to one hundred camels, among several of the tribes, and ratified by the

Wahabys, may be traced to the time of Abd el Motalleb Ibn Heshám (Mohammed's grandfather), who had made a vow to kill one of his ten sons in honour of the idol which was then worshipped in the Kaaba. The lot fell upon his favourite boy; but the intreaties of his friends, co-operating, we may suppose, with paternal affection, induced him to commute the sacrifice, and he immolated, in honour of the idol, one hundred camels, and this number thenceforward became necessary in atoning for blood. (See Azraky's History of Mekka.)

When a Bedouin of the tribes settled between Akaba and Cairo kills a man in blood-revenge, he exclaims, on cutting him down, "I take thy warm blood in revenge!" ناخد بثارنا دمك الساخن

No. IV.

The Catechism (or Creed) of the Wahabys. (See Vol. II. p. 104.)

Ibn Saoud to the inhabitants of Mekka the highly honoured.

Praise be to God, the only God! who has no co-partner—to whom belongs dominion, and who is omnipotent.

In the name of the all-merciful God! It is necessary that every chosen servant of God should have a true knowledge of the Almighty; for in the word of God (the Korán) we read, "Know that there is no God but one God!" *Bokháry*,* may God have mercy upon him! said, "First learn, then speak and act." If it be asked, "What are the three foundations of knowledge?" answer, "The servant's knowledge of his Lord, of his religion, and of his Prophet."

And first, as to the *knowledge of God*: if they ask of thee, "Who is thy Lord?" answer, "My Lord is God, through whose favour and grace I have been bred up; him I adore, and adore none but him." In proof of which we read (in the Koran), "Praise be to the Lord of all creatures! Whatever exists besides God, belongs to the class of creatures, and I myself am one of this created world." If they ask further of thee, "How didst thou know thy Lord?" answer, "By the signs of his omnipotence and the creation." In proof of which we read, "And of his signs are the night and the day, the sun and the moon; and of his creation, heaven and earth, and whatever is upon them and whatever they contain." And we likewise read, "Thy Lord is God, who created heaven

---

* The celebrated compiler of Mohammed's traditions.

and earth." If it be asked, "For what purpose did God create thee?" answer, "To adore him." In proof of this we read, "I created spirits and men to be adored by them." If it be asked, "What does God command?" answer, "The Unity; which means, to adore him exclusively and solely: and what he above all prohibits is the association with him, or the adoring of any other God besides himself." In proof of which we read, "Adore God, and do not associate with him any other thing or being." The adoration by which thou art to worship him, thou evincest by the *Islâm;* by faith and alms, by prayers, vows, sacrifices; by resignation, fear, hope, love, respect, humility, timidity, and by imploring his aid and protection.

In proof of the necessity of prayers we read, "Pray, and I shall grant your wishes." Prayers therefore are true adoration. In proof of the necessity of making vows we read, "Fulfil your vows and dread the day of which the evils have been foretold." To prove the necessity of slaughtering victims, we read, "Pray to God, and kill victims." And the Prophet, may God's mercy be upon him! said, "Cursed be he who sacrifices to any other but God."

The second foundation of knowledge is the *religion of Islâm*, which is submission to the

Almighty. In proof of which we read, "The religion before God is Islám" And to this refers the saying of the Prophet, on whom be the peace of God! "The chief of all business is Islám." If they ask, "How many are the principal duties of our religion?" answer, "They are three: Islám, faith, and good works." Each of these is divided into different parts:—Islám has five, viz. the profession that there is no God but God, and that Mohammed is his prophet—the performance of the prescribed prayers—the distribution of alms—the observance of the fast of Ramadhán, and the pilgrimage to the holy house of God. In proof of the truth of the *profession of faith*, we read, "God declares that there is no God but himself;" and the meaning of the expression "there is no God but God," confirms that there is but one God, and that nothing in this world is to be adored but God. And in proof of the profession, that Mohammed is the prophet of God, we read, "And Mohammed is nothing but a prophet." Our duty is to obey his commands, to believe what he related, to renounce what he forbade; and it is by following his precepts that we evince our devotion to God. The reason for joining these two professions, viz. in saying, "There is no God but God, and Mohammed is his prophet," is to show our piety and perfect obedience. In proof of *prayers and alms*, we read, " Nothing was commanded but that they should adore God, with the true religion alone, that they should perform prayers, and distribute alms." In proof of *fasts*, we read, " O ye true believers, we have ordained for you the fasts!" And in proof of the pilgrimage we read, " And God exacts the pilgrimage from those who are able to undertake the journey."

As a farther proof of these five fundamental parts of the *Islám*, may be quoted the tradition of Ibn Omar, who says, " The prophet, may God's mercy be with him, declared that the Islám rests upon five requisites: the prayers, the alms, the fast, the pilgrimage, and the profession that there is no God, but God." The second of the principal duties of religion, is the *faith*. It comprises seventy-nine ramifications.[*] The highest of them is the declaration, "There is no God, but God;" and the lowest, the removal of all deception from the road of the faithful. *Shame* (pudor) is one of those ramifications. The faith divides into six parts. These are: to believe in God and his angels, and the revealed books, and his prophets, and the last day, and the omnipo-

---

[*] The Arabic Ms. is not quite legible in this passage; it may be seventy-seven.

tence of God, from whom all good and evil proceed. In proof of which we read: "This is not righteousness, to turn your faces towards the east or the west;* but he is righteous who believes in God, and the last day, and the angels, and the sacred book, and the prophets." And in proof of the omnipotence, it is said: "We created every thing through our power." The third of the principal duties of religion consists in *good works*. These are comprised within one single precept, which is: "Adore God, as if thou didst see him; and if thou canst not see him, know that he sees thee." In proof of which we read, "He who turns his face towards the Almighty and confides in him, he is the well-doer, he holds fast by the firmest handle."

The *third* foundation of knowledge, is the *knowledge of our prophet Mohammed*, may God's mercy and peace be with him! Mohammed the son of Abdellah, the son of Abd el Motalleb, the son of Hashem, the son of Menaf, whose parentage ascends to Adnan, who was himself a descendant of Ismayl, the son of Ibrahím, with whom and with our prophet may God's mercy dwell! Mohammed, may God's mercy be with him! is a delegate whom we dare not adore, and

---

* Viz. to be exact in the ceremonial of praying.

a prophet whom we dare not belie; but we must obey and follow him, for it has been ordained to spirits and to mortals to be his followers. He was born and appointed prophet, at Mekka; his flight and his death were at Medinah. From him, to whom may God show his mercy! we have the saying: " I am the prophet, this is no false assertion, I am the son of Abd el Motalleb!" If it be asked, "Is he *a mortal?*" answer, "Yes; he is a mortal" In proof of which we read: "Say, I am but a mortal like yourselves, to whom it is revealed that your God is but one God." If it be asked, "*Is he sent to any particular class of mankind?*" answer, " No; he is sent to the whole race." In proof of which we read: " O men, I am God's prophet sent to you all!" If it be asked, "Can any *other religion, but his, be acceptable?*" answer, "No other can be accepted:" for we read, "Whoever shall follow any other religion than Islám, will be rejected." And if it be asked: " Does any *prophet come after him?*" answer, "No prophet comes after him; for after him comes the last day." In proof of which we read: "He was father to none of your men, but the prophet of God, and the seal (that is the last) of all prophets."

No. V

A Letter* of Mohammed Aly to the chief inhabitants of Medinah, acquainting them with the details of his great victory over the Wahábys, at Byssel. (January 1815.) (See Vol. II. p. 322.)

By the grace of the Most High!
To our worthy people, the inhabitants of Medinah the illustrious.

To the well worthy and noble primates, the neighbours of our prophet, (let God's mercy and peace be with him!) the first among the Sherffs and learned men, the praiseworthy, the venerable, the chiefs of the town, may God grant them his peace, take them under his care and custody, and pour out over them his full benevolence! Amen.

We give you our best salutation and greetings, and we announce to you that the Almighty, whose glory and power we celebrate, permitted us to accomplish the expectations of the Sultan of the

* This letter is a model of Arabic style. It was read before a general assembly in the great mosque of Medinah. (The original itself was in the possession of Mr. Burckhardt.)

Sultans of Islám, in prompting us to remove the army of true believers from Mekka, furnished with all necessary supplies of provisions, baggage, and ammunition, in order to transfer our head-quarters from thence to Kolach. We left for this purpose Mekka on Saturday the 26th of the month of Moharram, and arrived at Kolach on Wednesday, the last of that month. Our plan was to hasten towards Taraba, to encounter there the combined forces of the heretics, headed by their chief Faysal Ibn Saoud, accompanied by Ibn Shokban, Ibn Dohman, Ibn Katnan, and Ibn Mahy; also Bakhroudj and Ibn Hatamel, together with all the sheikhs of the Arabs of Beishe, and the Dowasir and Bekoom and Oteban Arabs, and those of the countries of Hedjaz, Sebya, and El Aredh. They had been, moreover, reinforced by Tamy and ten thousand of the Asyr Arabs, which increased their strength to the number of forty thousand men. The devil then beguiled their councils, and they intended to attack us. They left Taraba, and arrived in our neighbourhood, near the celebrated village of Byssel. We advanced against them with fifteen hundred of our horsemen, chosen from the number of true believers, and two field-pieces, in order to reconnoitre. At our approach, they spread over the mountains and offered determined resistance. But our soldiers devoted themselves to their duty, and after great slaughter, drove them back to their strongest holds.* We continued then under an incessant fire to attack them, and to endeavour to draw them into the plain. Our soldiers were engaged from sun-rise till sun-set. Night at last put a stop to the battle. We then took possession of the passes through which they might attempt their retreat. God sent us strength and stratagems.† We sent now for a reinforcement of two thousand foot-soldiers from Kolach, with their field-pieces, and again attacked the enemy at the break of day.‡ They did not stand our first attack, they flew, and God permitted our swords to be drenched in their blood. They abandoned their encampment, and upwards of five hundred tents, and five thousand camels, dromedaries as well as beasts of burden, with all the baggage and provisions fell a prey to our troops, who thus became masters of all their camp and all their honour.§ They pursued now the fugitives, who lost numbers, killed and

* The truth is, that on this first day the Turkish cavalry was repulsed.

† This is particularly well expressed in Arabic الي ان حال سننا الليل و لزمنا دروب فرارهم و بالله القوة و الحيل

‡ Nothing is said here of the Bedouins in the service of the Pasha, who were principal actors among the infantry.

§ A pun in Arabic; "camp and honour"—*Ordyhom* wa *Ardehom*, عرضيهم و عرضهم

taken prisoners; our allies the Arabs from Hedjaz likewise fell upon them in the narrow passes. Tamy himself escaped only with five horsemen and five camel-riders: God thus exterminated them by his power and strength. We left Kolaoh on Sunday, in hasty pursuit of the enemy, and arrived in the neighbourhood of Taraba on Tuesday. Faysal had taken refuge there with fifty horsemen and one hundred camel-riders, the remainder of his troops; but when he was apprised of our approach, he immediately fled. The people of Taraba, and the remaining part of its garrison, issued from the town to meet us and to beg for a safe-conduct. We promised to them security, and established our head-quarters in their town. All the neighbouring Arabs joined us here; and thus God permitted our wishes to be fulfilled in clearing these countries from their unjust and criminal oppressors. Let us address to him our most heartfelt thanks for the grace he has bestowed upon us, and the honour with which he covered our troops. If it please the Almighty, we shall leave this place in three or four days for Rannye and Beishe, and direct our march against the remaining Asyr Arabs, that we may establish order throughout the country, and destroy all rebels.

We wished to announce these good tidings, and

to inform you how the Almighty in his bounteousness has granted to us the accomplishment of all our hopes. May he complete his grace, and purify the whole country of Hedjaz from the filth of the wicked, by exterminating them. We charge you to pray for us at the tomb of our Lord, the Redeemer; and may the Almighty, in his gracious assistance, continue to regard you with kind looks! This is the matter of which we wished to inform you.

God's mercy and peace be with our Lord Mohammed, his family, and his followers!
On the 7th of the month of Safar,
1230 of the Hedjra.

(L. S.)

No. VI.

A Letter from Abdallah Ibn Saoud to Tousoun Pasha, upon occasion of the latter's departure from Kasym towards Medinah. (See Vol. II. p. 345.)

In the name of the all-merciful God!
Perfect peace, salutation, and honour to the Lord of Mankind, Mohammed, God's mercy and

best blessings be with him! and then to the noble Ahmed Tousoun Pasha, may God prompt him to godly works! And next, thy letter reached us, may thou reach God's good graces! And we rejoiced at the news of thy welfare and good health. As to what thou allegest in justification of thy demands, thou possessest understanding and penetration; and thou surely knowest that thy demands are inadmissible, and contrary to peace. If we did not wish to preserve a permanent and sincere friendship, and to fulfil the promises we once made, we should have granted thy demand. But we are men of faith and of truth, and we do not recede from conventions; and we execute them, were we even convinced of having been deceived. With regard to thy departure, we trust thou wilt not think badly of us, nor lend thine ear to our enemies, and to intriguing deceivers. Ask the Bedouins who are with thee, if they choose to speak the truth they will tell thee, that were they even to kill one of Saoud's own family, and that I had promised them safe-conduct, they would never doubt of it, but trust to my word. We tread here upon our own ground; this is our own country. Let us advise thee not to suspect our intentions, and to trust to our good faith. By God, and the pledges he gave to mankind, I promise not to molest either thee or thy armies in any manner that might be disagreeable to thee. Thou art placed under the safe-conduct of God, and of myself. At the moment thou breakest up upon thy return, I shall likewise break up, and retreat with my army towards Aeneyzy.* But if thou believest the reports of thy enemies, and suspectest our sincerity, we shall even now break up forthwith towards Aeneyzy; and do this for the deference we pay to thee and to thy father.† But we require that thou shouldest send us a letter pledging therein the safe-conduct of God, and of the Sultan, and thy own, to all the Arabs on our side, whether settlers or Bedouins. And a second letter of safe-conduct to the inhabitants of Shenanne, Betah, and Nebhanye,‡ which we shall immediately forward to them. If it please God, we shall to-night receive thy answer; therefore do not cause our man to tarry with thee. If thou likest to send camel-riders about the affair Ahmed mentioned to us, we shall have no objection. For all this we pledge to thee our faith before God.

Whenever it shall come to an amicable compromise, nothing will set the hearts of the Mos-

* A town of Kasym.

† Literally: to you and to the one who is behind you,
كرامة لخاطر كم و للي وراك

‡ Towns of Kasym.

lims* at rest, and tranquillize them, with regard to their whole party, but hostages to be sent to us. They will be under my protection; and at thy arrival at Dat,† they shall be sent back to thee; and thou shalt be well and honourably treated. Ibrahim will tell thee the names of these hostages: they are Mohammed Daly Bashy, Othman the Selehdar, Ismayl the Djokhadar, and Ahmed Aga. God's safe-conduct, and my own, is pledged to them. We shall cause them to be accompanied by some of our own people until they arrive at thy quarters. If they are sent to us, we shall, please God, forthwith break up. If on the contrary thou shouldst like to depart before us, we shall send to thee from our side hostages, who will follow thee. It is now for thee to choose. Either send us these people, and we shall depart, or start thyself, and take our own hostages. Let us have an answer to-day. We hope to God it will be such as to cause us joy. Be assured that the

* This expression is worthy of remark. The Wahabys call themselves by no other name but Moslims, (or true believers of the Islám,) distinguishing thus between themselves and the mere Turks. Here again, their party is called Moslims, which is as much as to say to the Pasha, " You are no Moslim." Perhaps it may be a mistake of the writer, as the letter, in its original, bears evident signs of great haste.

† Dat is the village of Kasym nearest towards Medinah.

hostages shall be under my special care. God's mercy and blessing be with Mohammed, his family, and his followers!

(L. S.)

From Abdallah Ibn Saoud.

INDEX OF ARABIC WORDS.

VOL. I.

PAGE
1. Aeneze, عنزه
3. Would Aly, ولد علي
4. El Teyar, الطيار—Meshadeka, مشادقا—Merreykhat, مرينخات—Lahhawein, لحوين Meshatta, مشطّا — Auadh, اواض Hammamede, حمامده
5. Djedaleme, حدالمه Tolouhh, طلوح—Hessenne, حسنه
6. Messaliekh, مسالخ Raualla, رولّا Djelaes, جلاس
8. Bessher, بشّر
10. Ahl el Shemál, اهل الشمال—Maualy, موالي
11. Hadedyein, حديديين

PAGE

12. Turkman, تركمان—Arab Tahht Hammel Hamáh, عرب تحت حمل حماه
14. Szoleyb, صليب
16. Feheily, فحيلي—Serdye, سردية
18. Ledja, لجا
19. Djolán, جولان
20. Kanneitera, قنيطرة
23. Beni Szakhr, بنى صخر
24. Abs, عبس
25. Belkaa, بلقا
26. Ghour, غور
29. Haueytat, حويتاط—Sherarat, شرارات
33. Dowar, دوار—Nezel, نزل — Fereik, فريق
34. Kabeile, قبيلة—Fende, فندة—Tayfe, طايفة—Beni, بني
35. Sulf, سلف
36. Medhour, مضهور—Dhaan, ضعن — Ghazou, غزو
37. Shauke, شوقة
38. Kheroub, خروب—Matrek, مترك—Sefife, سفيفة—Rowak, رواق
39. Sefale, سفالة—Mereis, مريس—Khelle, خلة
40. Kateaa, قاطع — Sáhhe, ساحة — Markoum, مرقوم—Redjoud, رجود
41. Roffe, رفة

ARABIC WORDS.

PAGE

43. Makszar, مقصر—Ketteb, كتب
45. Rawouye, راوية—Zeka, زكا — Udel, عدل—Harres, حرس
47. Mesoumy, مسومي — Meshlakh, مشلخ
50. Shauber, شوبر—Mekroune, مقرونه
51. Terkie, تركيه—Teraky, تراكي
52. Remahh san, رمح سان
53. Kennah, قناه — Harbe, هربه — Touman, تومان
55. Dora, درع
56. Kaldjak, قلجق—Dáfen, دافن
57. Lebs, لبس—Ftita, فتيته
58. Khafoury, خافوري — Ayesh, عيش — Behatta, بحته—Heneyne, حننه—Khubz, خبز—Sadj, صاج
59. Burgoul, برغل
60. Kemmáye, كمايه
61. Khelásy, خلاصي — Jebah, حماه Zebeídy, زبيدي
65. Szona, صنع
66. Oerk, عرق
68. Meghezel el souf, مغزل الصوف
72. Bakheil, بخيل
73. Wakhad helále, وخد حلاله

PAGE

78. Khádhere, خاضره
79. Nekhouet, نخوة
80. Koualeh, قواله
82. Asamer, اسامر — El kheil djeitna, &c.
الخيل جيتنا يا ديبا
الخيل جيتنا حطيبا
83. El kheil, &c. الخيل ضوحي يا دبا —Hodjeiny, حجيني
85. Szahdje, صهجه
86. Hadou, حدو
88. Moszana, مصنع
92. Sindián, سنديان
95. Hetout, حتوت
101. Welouloua, ولولوا
104. Zekawah, زكوه —Zeká, زكا
107. Talab, طلب —Kheteb, ختب
110. Ent tálek, انت طالقه
112. Tamehhe, طامحه
121. Mebesshae, مبشع
137. Metrás, متراس
195. Daly, دالي
230. Keffie, كفيه —Ares, ارس
233. Shebeyka, شبقه
237. Mezrak, مزراق — Orar el Deyghemy, عرار الديغمي

ARABIC WORDS.

PAGE

238. Mashhour, مشهور—Ftita, فتيته—Medjelleh, مجلله—Merekeda, مرقدد—Djereisha, جريشه—Nekaa, نقعه

240. Shyh, شيح—Kurs, قرص—Ayesh, عيش—Kahkeh, كهكه

243. Gharad, غرض—Dawíreh, دويره

244. Kahtan, قحطان

252. Rababa, رباب—Asamer, اسامر

254. "Get up, O camel," قوم يا جمل—"Walk fast," سوق—"The poor camel," &c. تعبان و عطشان—"Come and take," &c. قرب حتي نعلق لك

264. "None shall cover," &c. ما يغطك الا فولان

271. Ent taleka, انت طالقه

280. Rowadjeh, رواجه—Djaafere, جاعفره

290. Mebesshae, مبشع

293. Shahher, شحر—Djerba, جربه—Beney, بنيه

295. Agyd, عقيد

303. Kefyl, كفيل

312. "To dig up and to bury," الحفر و الدفن

314. Thar, ثار—Dye, ده—"Were hell-fire," &c. النار ولا نترك الثار

319. Hhasnai, حسناي

322. Wallahy inny ma, &c.

والله اني ما ثَقِّبتُ حلد
و ما يتمت ولد

INDEX OF

PAGE
323. Dhebahh, ذبح
328. Báikeh, بايقه
329. Zeben, زبن—Tezebbenet, تزبنت—Dakhelet, دخلت—Mezbene, مزبنه Melha, ملحه
335. Othman el Medhayfe, عثمان المضايفه El Medheyan, المضيّان
347. Abeyt, &c.

ابيت وحيد

و لا عند اولاد سعيد

355. Sheidje, شيجه — Syredje, سيرجه
366. Ghafeyr, غفير—Hasnay, حسناي — Hasneh, حسنه
369. Tayb, طيب
370. "May your day be white," نهارك ابيض— "May yours be like milk," نهارك لبن
371. "Ha, uncle," &c. يا عمنا الّي ماشي معكم اد والله يا خوي—"In truth," &c. موية مرحبابك
374. Athr, اثر
380. Djáhelye, حاهلية

VOL. II.

PAGE

1. Hessenne, or' Ahsenne, الاحسنه — Wády, وادي
2. Djelás, جلاس — Rowalla, روالة — Ktaysán, قتيسان — Doghama, دغمه — Feregge, فريقه — Naszyr, نصير —Omhallef, امحلف —Maadjel, معجل — Abdelle, عبدالله Fersha, فرشا—Bedour, بدور—Sowaleme, سوالمه
4. Tana Mádjed, طنا ماجد — Fedán, فدان Sebaa, سباع—Selga, سلقا
5. Djaafere, جعافره—Owadje, عواجه
6. Wayl, وايل
8. Howeytát, حويطات Atye, عطيه (plur. عطاونه) — Heywát, حيوات — Leheywát, لحيوات—Terábein, طرابين—Maazy, معازي —Tyaha, تياها
9. Moeyleh, مويلح — Hadnán, حدنان
10. Debour, دبور — Bedoul, بدول — Seyayhe, سيايحه — Hekouk, حكوك — Azázeme, عزازمه — Wahydát, وحيدات—Oulad el Fokora, اولاد الفقرة — Reteymát, رتيمات

INDEX OF

— Khanasera, خناسره Sowáleha, صوالحا

11. Sayd, صعيد —Owareme, عوارمه — Geráshy, قراشي—Gereish or Koreish, قريش — Rahamy, رحمي — Mezeyne, مزينه — Aleygát, عليقات
12. Wászel, واصل—Sherkyeh, شرقيه
13. Ayayde, عيايده — Salatene, سلاطنه—Djerabene, جرابنه—Maazy, معازي
14. Mowalle, (read *Mowaze*,) موازه — Ghanayme, غنايمه — Shedayde, شدايده — Zeráyne, زرعينه — Heteym, هتيم — Djeheyne, جهينه—Bily, بلي
15. Azayze, عزايزه—Amarat, عمارات
16. Hanády, حنادي
17. Howámede, حوامده — Oulad Mousa, اولاد موسي — Lebadye, لباديه
18. Megna, مقنع — Okaba, عقبه — Mesayd, مساعيد
19. Wodje, وجه — Bily, بلي in the sing. بلوي —Hassany, حساني
22. Abs, عبس (plur. عبوس)—El Harra, الحرّه
26. Shammar, شمّر—Degheyfat, دغفات
27. Djaafer, جعافر — Rebaay, رباعي—Orar el

ARABIC WORDS.

Deyghami, عرار الديغمي — Zegeyrat, زقيرات—Selga, سلقا

28. Sahhoun, سحّون—Zaab, زعب—Ageyl, عقيل
29. Zogorty, زقرتي—Djemamyel, جماميل
30. Meteyr, مطير — Alowa, علوي — Dowysh, دويش—Boráy, براي—Harabeshe, حرابشه —Borsán, برسان—Harb, حرب
32. Mezeyne, مزينه—Wohoub, وحوب — Gharbán, غربان—Djenayne, جناينه
33. Safar, سفر — Ammer, عمر — Fera, فرع Doýny, دويني—Hámede, حامده
34. Salem, سالم—Howáseb, حواسب—Sobh, صبح
35. Shokban, شقبان—Rehalát, رحالات—Khadhera, خضره—El Owf, العوف—Rábegh, رابغ
36. Haib, حيب — Dwy Dhaher, دوي ظاهر Ghor, غور—Zebeyde, زبيده
38. Sedda, سدّه — Djemmela, جمله — Saadyn, ساعدين—Ateybe, عتيبه (plur. عتبان)
39. Lahhyan, لحيان—Metarefe, مطارفه
40. Beni Fahem, بني فهم—Djehadele, جهادله— Dwy Barakat, دوي بركات — Koreysh, قريش
41. Ryshye, ريشيه — Kabákebe, كباكبه — Adouán, عدوان

PAGE

43. Harreth, حرّث —Thekyf, ثقيف —Hodheyl, هديل —Djebel Kora, جبل كرا

44. Alowyein, علويين —Nedowyein, ندويين — Beni Kháled, بني خالد — Toweyrek, طويرق Beni Sofyan, بني سفيان Modher, مُضر

45. Rabýa ربيعه —Ossoma, عُسمه —Begoum, بقوم

46. Oklob, أقلب —Sabýa, سبيعه —Salem, سالم —Kahtán, قحطان —Es-Sahama, السحامه —Gormola, قرمله —Aasy, عاسي —Dowáser, دواسر

47. Yám, يام —Okmán, عكمان —El Marra, المرة —Sad (or Saad), سعد

48. Nászera, ناصره — Málek, مالك — Ghámed, غامد —Zohrán, زهران —Shomrán, شمران —Asábely, عسابلي —Ibn el Ahmar, ابن الاحمر — Ibn el Asmar, ابن الاسمر —Beni Shafra, بني شفره — Asyr, عسير —Abyde, اييده — Senhán, سنحان — Wádaa, وادعه —Sahhár, صحار —Bagem, باقم

62. Thámerye, ثامريه

63. Nezahhy, نزحي —Keraye, قريه

64. "Go and wash the feet of your mare," &c. &c. اغسل رجليه الفرس و اشرب مويتها

PAGE

66. Birsim, برسيم
69. Om el Bel, ام البل
70. Djam, حعم
75. Hedjein, هجين
77. Osháry, عشاري (from عشر *ten*)
81. "His back is so soft," &c. ظهره لين تشرب عليه فنجان قهوه
82. "Will feed upon the fat of its own hump," ياكل في شحمه
84. Rás, راس—Ghabeit, غبط—Gissa, صعه
85. Shaghour, شغور Shaghaore, شغاور — Hawýe, حاويه — Shedád, شداد — Shebrýe, شبريه
86. Shekdef, شقدف—Takht raván, تخت روان
88. El Aasab, العصب — Fekek, فكك — Serrar, سرر — Hellel, هلل — Fáhoura, فاهوره —Sedreh khorban, صدره خربان
96. Abd el Waháb, عبد الوهاب
97. Temym, تميم — El Howta, الحوته Keffár, كفار
98. Messalykh, مسالخ
115. "Hateful," حكروه
121. Abou Showáreb, ابو شوارب
122. Faysal, فيصل—Nászer, ناصر—El Turky, التركي

INDEX OF

PAGE

138. Oulad es' Sheikh, اولاد الشيخ
146. "O doer," ما فاعل—"O leaver-off," ما تارك
153. Zeka, زكي
158. Nawáb, نواب— Mezekki, مزكّي Aámil, عامل
164. Sylle, سِلّة
165. Merádíf, مراديف
171. Mendjýeh, منجيه
173. El Sabr, السبر
176. Haret el Abasieh, حارت العباسه
177. Aman ullah, امان الله—Halka, حلقه
185. Thádj, ثاج
187. Zebeyr, زبير
188. Thoeny, ثويني— Szebeyhy, صبيحي El Koweyt, القويط
190. Abou Nokta, ابو نقطه—Othman el Medhayfe, عثمان المضايفه
193. Moabede, معبد
195. Abd el Mayen, عبد المعين—Ibn Name, ابن نعمه
197. Beni Sobh, بني صبح
206. Hark, حرك
208. Ras el Kheyme, راس الخيمه— Gowásim, (or Djowásin) قواسم
209. Refeydha, رفيضه

Printed in Great Britain
by Amazon